TRAPPING SECRETS

METHODS, TRICKS, AND TIPS OF A FIFTY-YEAR FUR TRAPPER

TRAPPING SECRETS

METHODS, TRICKS, AND TIPS OF A FIFTY-YEAR FUR TRAPPER

By

William Wasserman

ISBN 978-0-9718907-4-9

Also by William Wasserman

Poacher Wars: A Pennsylvania Game Warden's Journal

Wildlife Guardian: Stories of a Pennsylvania Game Warden

Game Warden: Adventures of a Wildlife Warrior

Pennsylvania Wildlife Tails: A Game Warden's Notebook

More Pennsylvania Wildlife Tails

Introduction

If there's one thing I've learned in a half-decade of trapping it's that although one trapper might catch tons of fur using certain lures and trapping methods, another trapper working just as hard in the same county, and using the same lures and methods, won't always have the same results.

If I knew why, I'd be basking in the sun on a private island in the Caribbean rather than writing this book right now. But having said that, it's vital to know that in order to be a successful trapper, you should be reading as many books and magazines about trapping as you can lay your hands on. Then extract the stuff that works best for you and run with it.

If you live in the Deep South but you're reading a book about mink trapping in Maine, you might want to eliminate the part about trapping under the ice. But that doesn't mean you won't pick up some valuable tips and techniques for catching mink in your own warmer climate.

The methods, sets, lures, and baits I've written about have brought me many years of success on the trapline. Some of them have never been seen in print before. It is my sincere hope and desire that this book will help you become a better trapper.

VI

Prologue

My 10-YEAR-OLD SISTER could see the excitement on my face as I hurried by. She was snuggled on the sofa, twisting a plastic ear into Mr. Potato Head. "Where are you going, Billy?" she asked.

I smiled back at her. "Trapping!" Then, scurrying out the door I added, "Tell Mom and Dad I'll be home soon!"

When I stepped outside, my brother, John, sighed with relief. He had been pacing the driveway, waiting anxiously for me to finish my morning chores. "Do you think we got one?" he asked excitedly.

"I hope so," I said. "Come on, I'll race you!" And with that, we dashed toward the Neshaminy Creek to check the traps we had set the day before.

It was November 1960. John F. Kennedy had recently been elected president in a close race against Richard M. Nixon; *Stay*, by Maurice Williams and the Zodiacs was America's number one song; and muskrats were king of the fur trade. It's hard to believe that more than a half century has passed since that day, but I remember it well: The bright, sapphire sky dappled with lazy white clouds; the sun, gentle and warm on our boyish faces; and the earthy scent of autumn leaves as we broke into the woods and raced toward the stream bank ahead. But most of all, I remember the heart-pounding, heady excitement that two 12-year-old boys felt as they were about to check a trap for the first time in their young lives.

The trap was a #1 Victor Jump that I had slipped into a deep, underwater den entrance by rolling up my shirtsleeve and reaching into the frigid stream as far as my arm could go. As it turned out, the trap was empty, but our spirits remained high as we continued to make our way along the meandering stream to check our remaining sets.

Muskrat sign was everywhere: slick trails, called slides, ran up and down the stream bank for as far as we could see. And gray, kidney bean shaped droppings were piled high on many of the logs and rocks that dotted the stream. Gazing into the water, we could tell where the muskrat dens were located by the "runs" that had been gouged into the stream bottom as the aquatic furbearers entered and exited their burrows deep below. Some runs were freshly clouded with muddy water, telling us that a muskrat had recently been there, which made it even more difficult to bear when our foothold traps would come up empty, time and again, as the muskrats swam right over them.

John and I had purchased the traps for 25 cents apiece from a friend named Lance, whose father had used them years ago. Hoping Lance would know how to get the muskrats to step into our traps, I sat across from him during lunch at the school cafeteria the following day and waited patiently as the stocky farm boy wolfed down a huge plate of raviolis, mashed potatoes, green beans, and peach slices (all for only 35 cents). As soon as he finished eating, I asked him how in the world his father managed to catch muskrats in the traps he'd sold us.

Lance took a big gulp from his milk carton, wiped his mouth with the back of his hand, and belched vociferously. "Oh those things," he said with a wrinkled brow. "My dad caught most of his muskrats in Conibears, not jump traps!"

"*Conibears?*" I shot back in bewilderment. "What are they?"

"Killer traps," shrugged Lance. "You stick 'em in front of the den hole and when the muskrat swims through the trap it kills them instantly."

This sounded like the perfect solution to my problem. I couldn't wait to get my hands on one. "I have a dollar!" I offered, reaching into my pocket to fish it out. "How many will that buy?"

8

Lance stuck out his meaty hand and I dropped the wrinkled bill into it. "Tell you what, take the school bus home with me and I'll sell you two Conibears that are like new."

"Deal!" I said eagerly.

Lance looked across the table and eyed the peanut butter and jelly sandwich my mom had packed for me. "Gonna eat that?"

I'd been so focused on talking about trapping that I had forgotten all about it. "Guess not," I said pushing the sandwich his way. Besides, my appetite had dwindled considerably after watching him practically inhale his own lunch.

While on the school bus with Lance, I hammered him with questions about how to trap. He had very little experience himself, having accompanied his father only on rare occasions while trapping muskrats. But he managed to give me a few good tips on how to use Conibear traps, and he also told me how to make drowning sets when using foothold traps. When we got off the bus at his farm, he motioned me to follow him into the barn where several dozen rusted traps hung on a wall. Lance pulled two Conibears from the tangled assortment and handed them to me. Then we walked over to an old wooden desk and he opened the top drawer and pulled out a paper catalog. "Take this," he said solemnly. "I want you to have it."

I reached out and took the pamphlet from his hand. It said *O. L. Butcher's Trapping Supplies, Shushan, New York.* "He's a professional trapper," Lance remarked with a reassuring nod. "Before my father died, he talked about him all the time."

"Geez thanks," I exclaimed. "This looks really neat!" Then I saw his eyes start to water up and his chin begin to quiver, and I felt terrible. Lance was a big kid, and I knew he didn't want me to see him cry, so I looked down at my Timex wristwatch ("Takes a Licking and Keeps on Ticking") and pretended that I had to go. "Wow! It's late. My Mom is gonna kill me!" Then I turned and ran away as fast as my legs could carry me. Looking back, I guess I was running away from myself more than anything. I still had a father, and it frightened me to think about what it would be like if he died as Lance's dad had.

Lance didn't know it, but he changed my life forever that day. After I got tired of running, and started walking toward home, I began thumbing through the catalog and dreamed of becoming a professional trapper like Mr. Butcher. There was a picture of him on the cover: a husky, rugged looking man wearing a checkered shirt and knit cap as he sat on a stump by his log cabin. Dozens of fox and beaver pelts lined the exterior wall behind him, and he became an instant hero to me.

Back home, I showed my brother the catalog and the new traps I had purchased. Excited about the prospect of finding fur in our traps, John began paging through the catalog and soon found an advertisement for a book called *The Trappers Guide*, written by O. L. Butcher. "We have to get a copy of this book!" he declared.

"Yeah, that would be cool!" I said. "But I just gave Lance two weeks allowance for two traps. I'm broke!"

"Don't worry, I'll pay for it," said John. "Fair is fair, and since you bought the traps, I'll buy the book." So, we borrowed a four-cent stamp from Mom's kitchen drawer (it had a picture of a Pony Express cowboy riding hard on it), licked it good and stuck it on an envelope along with a dollar bill and a short note to Mr. Butcher asking him about his life as a professional trapper.

Muskrats were the schoolboys' meal ticket back in those days. They were everywhere. Small creeks running through cornfields provided excellent food and cover for them, and local farmers happily granted us permission to trap the voracious furbearers. Some streams were infested with them, and damage to the banks caused by their constant tunneling was dramatic. Nevertheless, my brother and I had but a handful of traps and were only allowed to set them on weekends while school was in. As a result, we did little to help control the burgeoning muskrat populations.

But things began to change when we received O. L. Butcher's book. My brother and I were doing homework at the kitchen table when our mother suddenly walked in with a manila envelope in her hand and a smile on her pretty face. "Guess what came in the mail today, boys," she said.

John and I both looked up and grabbed for the package at the same time. "Ah, ah, ah!" Mom cautioned. "Homework comes first.

Needless to say, we finished our homework in record time and soon found ourselves tearing open the package from O. L. Butcher. We were delighted to see that he had sent us a hand-written letter along with his book. I have kept it, along with several others he sent me before he passed away in 1967. In his letter, he wrote:

Dear Bill and John,

I trap for a living and will start after cats and brush wolves for $25 bounty soon after Labor Day. Then will trap mink, rats, fisher, coon, and fox as soon as the season opens. Last spring I trapped 68 beaver and 4 otter — one beaver for each year I am old.

I didn't see that going trapping as a profession was always a poor mans occupation. Only occasionally are furs up to where one makes good wages. But furs will always be in demand as long as pretty girls are—

Thanks, Butch

John and I were thrilled. After all, we were only twelve, and O. L. Butcher *himself* had actually written a letter to us! Gee whiz, he was one of the best trappers in the whole world! His catch of 68 beavers astounded us. And his plans to trap exotic furbearers like brush wolves (eastern coyote) and fishers in the remote Adirondack Mountains of New York had our hearts pounding with unbridled envy.

My brother and I pored through his book, eyes like saucers as we examined the exciting photographs taken from his wilderness traplines. We read every word, studied every set, and memorized every secret the master trapper had revealed. By the time we stopped reading, it was long past our bedtime. But tomorrow was Saturday, and our parents had allowed us to stay up late so we could finish our new book. Excited by all we had learned, I finally turned out the lights and drifted off to sleep, dreaming of meandering streams in faraway places and trapping muskrats by the hundreds.

At precisely 6:00 a.m. the following morning, my clock radio came alive to the tune of Elvis (The King) Presley singing his latest hit, *It's Now or Never*. John and I leaped out of our beds, slipped into faded dungarees, and tiptoed quietly downstairs so as not to awaken our family. After a quick bowl of Sugar Pops and milk, we grabbed our jackets and rubber boots, and hustled into the garage to get some traps.

As we proceeded toward the creek, armed with our newfound knowledge, I looked at my brother and said, "I think this is the day we become real trappers!"

John glanced at me with a mischievous grin. Then he threw back his head and bellowed, *"IT'S NOW OR NEVVVERRR,"* in one of the worst imitations of Elvis I ever heard. I tried not to laugh; but more I tried, the harder it was to succeed. I could feel my chest start to shake, and then my lips began to flutter, and before I knew it I had a severe case of the giggles. Then we both burst out laughing so hard our bellies started to ache, which made the long walk to Neshaminy Creek go by twice as fast.

We set six traps that day. But the following morning our traps were all empty, their jaws gaping back at us in mute testimony. We were disappointed, but John and I refused to give up. We continued to set our traps each weekend until we finally caught our first muskrat, its rich brown fur glistening like polished walnut in the early morning sun.

I will never forget those early days on the trapline with my brother, John. We shared a sense of adventure few our age could know. Being in the woods and streams, alone, away from human dwellings, scouting for fur, was an indescribable joy. We often imagined ourselves as pioneers—the first to set foot wherever we happened to be!

Trapping transformed our lives in many ways, and we began to mature into men that winter so long ago. Through trapping, we learned about responsibility: when traps are set, they must be checked every day. That was a moral and ethical obligation. Some mornings we would step outside and the cold wind would take our breath away. The temptation to retreat back into the cozy warmth of our home was great, but the allure of the trapline with its curious mysteries and rousing surprises was far greater, and we would stride into the early darkness with our handful of traps in search of adventure.

John and I not only learned about *how* to trap that winter, we also learned a lot about *why*. We discovered that trapping wasn't about making money—it wasn't even about catching fur, really. It was about learning to read sign, like animal tracks and scats; it was about matching wits with animals on their own turf; it was about animal behavior, lures and scents, proper skinning and care of pelts, grading fur; it was about ethics, responsibility, self-respect, purposefulness, and rugged individualism.

Yes, my twin brother and I got quite an education that first season on the trapline, fifty years ago, and our love for trapping managed to keep us out of trouble while growing up. It also fostered a deep appreciation for our commonwealth's natural resources, which eventually led both of us into careers as Pennsylvania wildlife conservation officers.

John and I still find time to trap these days, and the trapline continues to teach us things about life. Even now.

Efficient Water Trapping

WE OFTEN HEAR about trappers who catch more fur in a single season than most of us dream of taking in a lifetime.

What is it that makes them so successful? Could it be a secret lure or bait so potent that it draws every mink, beaver, or muskrat into their traps for miles around? Perhaps it's a secrete set kept hidden from our knowledge, a set that can't be passed up, even by the wariest of furbearers.

While it's true that lures, baits, trap placement, and set location all play important roles in producing large fur catches, today's trappers aren't holding back many secrets. In fact, most of the best trapping techniques have been written about time and again. Truth be known, the blueprint for a successful trapline boils down to a combination of advanced planning, simple sets, and hard work.

Trappers who consistently out-perform everyone else in their territory do so because they have a strategy. They work smart in addition to working hard. They know that the key to success on any trapline is efficiency, which adds up to working effectively with a minimum of waste, expense, or unnecessary effort.

Of course, in order to catch a lot of fur, you must have a large population of furbearers in your area. And in order to determine if you do, it's best to spend time scouting prior to the opening bell. Summer months are an ideal time to pick up new territory. Days are longer, which gives us ample time to visit landowners and ask permission to trap after clocking out at our regular jobs. In early autumn, you should be checking these newfound trapping areas for fresh sign. Established territories should also be given the once-over prior to opening day; otherwise, we risk wasting time, money, and energy by traveling to areas lacking an essential quantity of fur.

Some of us are so busy dealing with our regular jobs and families that we barely have time to set traps, let alone prospect for fur. I've experienced those times in my life but still managed to evaluate most of my trapping grounds simply by checking under the bridges on my traplines. Often a quick glance will tell you if beavers are living upstream because fresh cuttings will invariably be seen along the bank. A rough estimate of mink, muskrat, and raccoon populations can also be established by the tracks and droppings found under bridges.

Often, beaver dams can be observed right from the road, and a trapper can determine if the dam is "live" by doing a quick visual inspection. Binoculars can help if the dam is distant. In fall, active beaver lodges will often have fresh mud packed upon them as these giant rodents keep their homes in a constant state of repair. Also, freshly peeled sticks, bright white and visible from afar, will be evident in the water around the lodge and dam

Another way to quickly determine fur populations is by talking to the landowner. Most are intimate with their surroundings and can provide you with a wealth of knowledge about the mink, muskrats, beavers, otters and other furbearers that inhabit the area.

I've had landowners point out holes and crevices where they've seen mink and muskrats disappear that I might never have noticed. These same places often turn out to be virtual hot spots where every mink and muskrat inhabiting the waterway can be caught with a single trap. Boat docks are a prime example. I've never met a landowner that didn't tell me he sees lots of muskrats, as well as an occasional mink, under his boat dock. Boat docks offer muskrats shelter and the freedom to congregate while being protected from avian predators. A few well-placed traps here can reduce an entire muskrat population in short order.

The author O. Henry had a famous line in his 1908 book *The Gentle Grafter*, which applies to today's modern trapper: "It was beautiful and simple as all truly great swindles are," he wrote. Be assured that the best trappers keep their sets and methods simple too. And therein lies the beauty of a successful and efficient trapline.

Fancy or elaborate sets may have their place, but if you want to catch a lot of fur, you must set lots of traps. This is only possible through advanced preparation and by keeping your sets uncomplicated. You should strive to place traps in areas that serve as conduits for furbearers. These can be structures like bridges, road culverts, and beaver dams, or artificial places created by the trapper.

Bridges and road culverts are key locations for trappers who wish to save time but still cover acres of territory. Because they act as funnels for aquatic furbearers, they can be a virtual gold mine to trappers.

Trappers making large catches often place more than a single trap or two at these areas. When setting up wide bridges, keep in mind that mink like to hug walls, so it's advisable to have at least one trap on each side of the bridge. Additional baited traps, serving as combination sets targeting both mink and raccoons, should lie near each end of the structure.

Muskrats also frequent bridges and culverts; therefore, an additional trap or two should be devoted solely to catching them. When good trap locations are scarce, I create a pair of fake muskrat slides by rubbing two swaths into the soft bank with my boot and bed a trap at the base of each one.

I often catch muskrats this way, as they are attracted to the fresh mud. A piece of apple pushed into the bank can improve the set dramatically.

I seldom use lures for mink. Again, I like to keep things simple, and a good bait is all that is necessary. Contrarily, I rarely use bait for muskrats but have found apples work best when I do.

When trapping stone bridges I'll take a hunk of muskrat meat or fish, push it into an opening in the wall between two stones, and set a trap in front of it. The set only takes a few seconds to make and is one of my favorites for mink and raccoons. Solid cement bridges and steel road culverts generally don't offer cracks in which to place your bait, but they can be set up just as quickly by placing your bait on a flat rock approximately the size of a dinner plate that sits just above the water line. Place your bait on the center of the rock and cover the bait with a similar sized rock. Then bed your trap alongside it and you will have a set that will take mink and raccoons as they circle the rock in an attempt to locate a free meal.

The only trap I use when setting at bridges and road culverts (unless I'm trapping beavers) is a 1-½ coil spring attached with six feet of chain. Things are a lot less complicated when you don't have to dig around for a different trap every time you make a set. The setup I use will hold raccoons, mink, and muskrats, and will drown the latter two in seconds due to the combined weight of trap and chain. The chain ends are equipped with a quick link (a chain link with a threaded bushing that opens and closes the link) so I can attach either a pronged coyote grapple or railroad plate to my trap.

Grapples and drags are an efficient way to secure water traps because they save the time and energy involved with pounding stakes through rocky stream bottoms and eliminate the problems associated with securing traps in loose sand and mud. The 1-½ coil spring takes a high hold on both mink and 'rats preventing them from footing out. They also have tremendous holding power. When coupled with a chain and drag they are unbeatable for raccoons because once the coon tangles up he forgets about his foot in the trap (raccoons are chewers), and spends most of his time fighting the surrounding brush.

And don't worry about spending a lot of time looking around for your trap after a catch is made. Mink and muskrats won't move your rig much at all, and raccoons will usually be within 20 feet of where your trap was set. As soon as your trap clamps on a raccoon's foot it will instinctively jolt back, in the opposite direction of its approach, to get away from what has just grabbed hold of it. Look toward the brush behind where your trap was set and you'll usually find a masked marauder waiting there for you.

If there isn't any brush to tangle in, I attach my chain to a railroad plate. Twenty pounds of abandoned iron is heavy enough to keep even the brawniest raccoon from traveling very far. Simply attach your trap chain to one of the holes found at each end of the plate. After the season ends, I leave my railroad plates at the set location which eliminates the unnecessary burden of hauling them around with me year after year. Railroad plates are also effective when making drowning sets. Again, I often leave the plate at the set location after pulling my trap and drowning cable.

When I have to walk any distance to catch beavers, I find it much easier to use a burlap bag filled with rocks gathered at the set location as a drowning device. I only use drowning sets when trapping beavers, and then only if I can't catch them in a bodygrip trap or snare. In other words, I won't resort to foothold traps for beavers unless I'm dealing with a trap shy flattail that refuses to enter my more efficient bodygrippers or snares.

I always have a generous supply of drowning rigs on hand that I assemble with snare cable in various lengths during the off-season. I run the cable through a drowning lock and use double ferrules to make small permanent loops at each end (more on snaring later in this book). This way, when I'm on the trapline, all I need do is grab the appropriate length cable and attach my trap (which is on a short chain) to the drowning lock. One looped end of the cable is for my stake, the other gets fastened to whatever I'm using for a weight at the stream bottom.

If you're using railroad plates, one will usually be sufficient for even the most powerful beaver if caught in deep water, especially if the plate settles into the muddy stream bottom, making movement difficult at best. If caught by a front foot, the beaver is held at the plate with almost no leverage, while a hind foot catch leaves but one webbed foot to paddle with.

One of the most important tools I've found for efficient water trapping is a good shovel. Mine was designed for digging up trees. It has a 28-inch handle with a blade that measures 5-inches wide by 14-inches long. The shovel is strong and durable. It can be used in place of a walking stick on unstable surfaces and works great for digging pocket sets or carving up a stream bank in order to steer mink, muskrats, raccoons, and beavers into your traps. It can also be used to fish traps out of murky waters, dispatch trapped animals, and as a pry bar or lever when necessary.

Railroad plate and shovel used on my water traplines.

Beaver dams are second only to bridges and road culverts for drawing furbearers. Mink inspect beaver dams regularly to hunt for small mammals hiding in the tangle of sticks. A careful inspection will also reveal where mink regularly cross over the dams as they travel along the stream. Otters do this too. In fact, everything from foxes to fishers can be found nosing around beaver dams, and they will often use them as a bridge to access the opposite side of the pond.

Bodygrip traps are always best for beavers and muskrats. These traps can be set in seconds, don't have to be anchored as securely as snares or footholds, and the critter is dead when you arrive. Bodygrip traps are a primary resource for speed and efficiency on the water trapline.

When you want high numbers of 'rats, nothing beats plunking a bodygripper in front of an underwater den entrance. The trap can be set and staked in no time, and you don't have to worry about foot-outs. However, foothold traps have their place, and when I use them for 'rats, I often use Victor Stoploss traps. The dollar apiece extra you spend on these traps will pay for itself a hundred times over. In a lifetime of trapping, I have never lost a single muskrat caught in one of these traps, and that includes muskrats caught and held alive on land.

When trapping beavers, my bodygrip traps are rigged for efficiency by removing the chains and equipping them with six feet of snare cable ending in a ¾-inch chain snap (often used at the end of a dog leash). The chain snap enables me to attach my trap to almost anything. I can run a rerod bar through the eye and stake it solid or wrap my cable around a clump of saplings and hook the snap back on the cable to cinch it like a noose. Chain snaps cost about a buck apiece, but it's money well spent. When packing your traps, fold the springs in and wrap your cable around the jaws several times, then latch the chain snap onto a jaw or spring to make everything easy to stow.

When I encounter trap shy beavers on my line, I don't spend much time fooling with them unless the landowner wants every beaver removed from his property. Even then, I'll move on to other locations first and expend my time and energy catching the more cooperative flattails before the weather turns nasty and my catch begins to drop off.

When things slow down, I begin to work on the beavers I missed earlier. These wise old flattails are often very difficult to catch and will avoid bodygrip traps no matter how you try to conceal them. That's when I bring out my snares. I've caught a lot of beavers in snares over the years, but they require a bit more time and effort than bodygrip traps, so I rarely use them on my regular trapline. However, snares will take most trap shy beavers and are often more efficient than foothold traps.

The strategies and techniques in this chapter have enabled me to become a more efficient water trapper over the years. If you give them a chance, I'm sure they'll work well for you too.

FINDING FUR UNDER THE ICE

WHEN I GOT the complaint about muskrats and beavers wreaking havoc at a pond on a local farm, the ice was already two inches thick.

I was familiar with the pond and knew about its treacherous shoreline. Muskrat dens were difficult to find here because of the steep, weedy banks and blackish water. But the ice would make things easier for me. I'd have a solid shelf to walk on and telltale bubbles that would lead me to every active den.

Even as I approached the pond from a distance, I could see where some of the muskrats were frequenting. A 12-inch circle of open water along the icy shoreline indicated muskrat activity and the likelihood of a den under the bank. Closer scrutiny revealed small pieces of root and other vegetation floating about. The water was cloudy, too, indicating that the muskrats had been feeding here just minutes ago.

I slipped a booted foot into the murky water, probed around a bit with my toe, and found a den entrance. Taking a size 110 Conibear from my five-gallon supply bucket, I guarded the hole with my trap, its single long spring jutting straight up. Next I pushed a wooden stake through the spring's ringed end and on into the soft bank in a 45 degree angle. I made sure that the stake pressed down on the spring, forcing the base of my bodygripper against the bottom to stabilize the trap.

Moving on, I soon located another likely 'rat den. From under the grassy bank, I could see a thick mass of air bubbles beneath the ice. They trailed out in two directions, traveling several feet until finally tapering off in deep water. Here the ice was thinner too. I knelt down and peered through the glassy surface at the den entrance below. There was a deep run carved into the pond bottom, perfect for a trap or two. I gently tapped the ice with a gloved hand and broke through, then pushed the floating shards aside and eased two more Conibears into the pond. I secured each of them with a single wooden stake as before. One trap covered the den entrance while the other was placed directly into the muskrat's run a few feet away.

Most of the wooden stakes I use for muskrat trapping come from beaver ponds. Discarded remnants from their feeding areas, the peeled sticks not only make great stabilizers for small bodygrippers but can be used for bracing or fencing off larger bodygripping traps for beavers too. If not too old and discolored, they also make great guide sticks for beaver traps because the absence of bark makes them stand out under the dusky waters found on many traplines.

I continued to set traps, pinpointing den after den simply by locating thick columns of bubbles trapped under the ice and following them back into the bank. Within an hour, I had set more than a dozen bodygrippers and had every muskrat den covered.

The beaver lodge was my last stop. It was built on the edge of the pond with its entrance under three feet of water. I could see a massive swarm of bubbles arcing out in a broad swath under the ice, revealing exactly where the beaver was exiting the lodge through a jumble of sticks. I broke away a large section of ice and searched for a suitable trap location. There was a log jutting straight out from the bottom of the lodge. It ran for several feet and helped form the base of the lodge. The log would make a perfect guide for my bodygripper, as it formed the edge of the beaver's runway.

I opened the jaws of a number 330 Bodygripper and pushed the springs in two different directions. The one that would shoulder the log ran straight up at a 90-degree angle, the opposite spring was pushed down at a 45-degree angle so it would touch the bottom of the pond and help stabilize the trap. I slowly lowered my bodygripper until it was nestled alongside the log. The icy water was deep enough so that it almost entered the top of my shoulder gauntlet, making things a bit difficult, but I managed to set the trap exactly where I wanted it.

I pushed the trap's trigger from the center to the side so the beaver would have a clear, unobstructed path as it left the lodge. If a beaver slows down to investigate your trap, it might get spooked and decide to turn back. The beaver's sudden about-face could cause its tail to strike a trap jaw or one of the springs, setting it off. Once this happens, the beaver will likely be trap shy.

With my trap balancing itself precariously in front of the beavers escape hole, I eased a stake between the top jaws at the upper corner and on into the ground just enough keep the trap from tipping over. The stake was temporary, and in a 45-degree angle to the trap. Its job was to hold the bodygripper steady until sprung by a beaver. Once the jaws closed, the trap would fall free. Ten feet of attached cable would allow the beaver's momentum to carry it away from the lodge so it wouldn't spook the other residents.

I've always been able to successfully trap muskrats and beavers in areas that I'm totally unfamiliar with by locating air bubbles under the ice. The only downside is that the method is so productive that you must be careful not to wipe out an entire population. Try these methods for yourself, and I'm sure you will be happy with the results.

BEAVER TALK

As BEAVER PONDS GO, it was the smallest I'd ever seen. Although the dam was impressive enough, the water behind it was no bigger than a basketball court. A medium-sized beaver lodge sat on the far bank, and by the looks of everything, I guessed a solitary beaver had moved in.

The township wanted the beaver removed because it kept plugging up a road culvert just downstream of the dam I was glad to accommodate them. Figuring I'd be out within a day or so, I pulled a size 330 from my truck and approached the dam. Grabbing several loose logs from the dam breast, I arranged them in a V with the opening toward the water. My trap guarded the passage with a nice green poplar placed behind it. I pushed a second poplar in front of the bodygripper to get Mr. Beaver's appetite going in case he had reservations about sticking his head into my trap.

The following morning, I discovered that the beaver was trap shy. The bait stick ahead of the trap had been taken but the beaver refused to enter my bodygripper to get the second poplar branch. I knew it was useless to try coaxing him in. If a beaver won't enter a bodygripper the first time, he's not apt to change his mind later. Trap shy beavers can make a fool out of the best trappers. Of this, I was certain, because they were still making a fool out of me.

With that in mind, I switched to a set that had produced many shy beavers over the years. Taking a green poplar branch two inches in diameter, I hammered it securely into the water at the bank's edge. A beaver could not simply carry it off; he would have to work on it for a while. And this was the beauty of my set. Eventually, Mr. Beaver would have to set his hind feet down in order to get a firm grip on the bait. Two number four double coilsprings were waiting there, twelve inches apart and eighteen inches deep, ready to grab a large webbed foot.

When I checked my trap the next day, I had a blanket beaver waiting for me. At first, I thought my job was done, another beaver problem solved for the township. But a closer look revealed that the bait stick had been eaten all the way to the ground. Surely the beaver at the bottom of my slide wire hadn't done it. There had to be another.

I reset my foothold traps and placed a baited bodygripper nearby. I wanted an additional trap available, and the bodygripper was fast and easy compared to running another drowning rig with footholds. If two beavers were living in the lodge, there was a good chance several young would be too.

The following day, I had another large beaver at the bottom of the pond, and the bait was missing again, which told me there was at least a third beaver in the tiny pond. The bodygripper I had set nearby was untouched, although the small poplar stick I'd placed in front of it was gone. Once again, a beaver had refused to enter the bodygripping trap.

I reset the drowning rig and hammered in a fresh poplar branch. I hadn't thought I'd catch more than one beaver in the tiny pond. Now I was after number three! As I drove off, I couldn't help but wonder how many beavers lived in the lodge, and why it was that none of them would enter my bodygripper.

The following morning I had a drowned beaver in my foothold trap and the bait had been eaten again. I checked my bodygripper and the poplar stick in front of the trap had been stolen again. This meant at least four beavers were in the pond, and each had avoided entering my bodygripper. I started to wonder if beavers could talk to each other.

I continued to catch a beaver every day in my foothold set until I had a grand tally of eight from the lodge: two large, two medium, and four small. The thing that amazed me was that every single beaver, including the small ones born last spring, had refused to enter a bodygripping trap. I've caught many beavers in bodygrippers and have cleaned out entire colonies (in complaint areas) without encountering a shy beaver. But in this case, the entire colony had steered clear of my traps.

I had an incident with beavers later that season that showed me how this can occur. I was trapping near a beaver lodge while a medium-sized beaver swam around watching me as I set three bodygripping traps baited with poplar and lured with beaver castor.

I decided to double back an hour after setting my traps, thinking I'd probably have the beaver. When I returned, there were three beavers swimming near the traps and sniffing the air as they paddled along. A large male was in the lead. He swam back and forth near my castor mound smacking his broad tail in the water with great force.

After watching from a distance for a half-hour, I drove off and returned the following day expecting all three beavers would be caught. But I only had the big male. The other bodygrippers were empty, and the bait had been stolen from behind them. Apparently, the others had watched the first beaver get caught, and that was all it took to smarten them up. Afterwards they absolutely refused to enter a bodygripper. What's worse, they would approach a trap and slap their tails in the water with such vigor that the trap would snap shut. Only after springing the trap, would they move in and take the poplar bait. I am certain, had they not witnessed the demise of the first beaver, each would have easily been captured.

I had long known that most beavers are not afraid of traps until they have a bodygripper slam shut in their face or get a toe pinched in a foothold trap. But seeing these beavers learn to fear bodygripping traps after watching their mate get caught gave me a new appreciation for a beaver's mental capabilities.

Fortunately, I rarely experience this problem with foothold traps. One prime example is the eight beavers I wrote about earlier that had refused to enter a bodygripper while each became caught in foothold traps. I'm not saying a beaver can't be shy of these traps too. They most certainly can. But they usually don't learn this fear after seeing another beaver getting caught in one, as they do with bodygrippers. The foothold trap is relatively silent as it grips the beaver's foot, and since most are set with a drowning rig, the captured animal immediately dives to the bottom where it stays put; consequently, other beavers rarely become alarmed.

Snares are another excellent way to capture trap shy beavers (check state game laws for legality). I've taken many beavers in snares that wouldn't venture anywhere near a bodygripping trap. Because a snare doesn't snap shut, but instead closes softly, beavers usually don't fear them even if they manage to spring one without being caught.

There was an exception to that rule this past season. I had placed a bodygripper with a poplar stick behind it in a dead end channel that intersected the main watercourse. The beavers were trap shy and would crawl out of the channel to walk around the trap, only to enter the channel again and steal the poplar stick. Interestingly, once they had the bait, they'd immediately forget about the bodygripper and swim right through it on the way back to their lodge. I'd find both the beaver and my bait stick caught in the trap the following day (evidently, beavers can't think about two things at once). But after catching several beavers this way, I ran into one that refused to come near the trap. I tried camouflaging the bodygripper, but the beaver couldn't be fooled.

Eventually, I replaced the bodygripper with a snare, thinking I'd have the beaver on my next trip. But still the beaver refused to swim up the channel to the poplar stick, while any bait that I placed ahead of the snare was taken.

I checked my set daily for a week, waiting for the beaver to overcome his fear of my dangling wire, but it was useless. Ol' flattail was not about to trade his hide for a succulent sapling no matter how enticing.

It was quite by accident that I happened upon the answer. The weekend approached, and I planned to be out of town, so I pulled the snare but left the bait and the wooden stake that secured the snare in place. When I returned, I was surprised to see that the bait had been untouched the entire time! Why? There was no trap or snare to frighten him.

Suddenly it dawned on me: when I replaced my bodygripper with a snare, I supported it with the same wooden stake I'd used to stabilize the bodygripper that had captured its mates. Consequently, the beaver regarded the wooden stake as something to avoid. I had to replace it with something. So, after laying big rock parallel to the channel for a base, I attached a heavy-gauge wire and used it to support my snare. It was simple and easy. And the following morning I had a blanket beaver waiting for me.

A Beaver Tale

I**T ALL STARTED OUT** routinely enough. I was called by a landowner to get rid of the beavers invading his property. At first, he'd been happy to see them move in. But the novelty soon wore off as the voracious rodents began eating everything in sight. They had even girdled a number of half-century-old oaks. The trees would soon die, and the farmer didn't want to lose any remaining hardwoods.

He was also concerned about a heavy wooden bridge he'd built. It spanned a narrow stream between two beaver dams, and he was afraid it would soon be submerged by rising water as the beavers continuously added to the size of their dams.

No problem, I assured him. The nuisance beavers would be exterminated in a matter of days.

He was elated.

And at first, all went rather well. I could drive right down to the bridge and unload my truck. From there, it was a short walk to the main dam, and I managed to put in four good sets in an hour. The January day was sunny and mild, the skies blue and the beavers plentiful. Life didn't get any better than this.

The next day found me up early to check my sets. Since no one had been trapping here before, I didn't expect any problems with shy beavers. But that notion was soon to be shattered.

My first trap held a large beaver lured into a 330 bodygripper baited with poplar. The trap was set in front of an old beaver crawl out that I'd freshened by slicking up the bank with a booted foot. The poplar stick I'd used as bait had been peeled just enough to catch the eye of a passing beaver and pushed into the indented bank a few inches behind my trap.

My next two traps held beavers caught in what I call teepee sets. I gathered a quick armload of loose sticks floating near the dam and laid them on the bank, one atop the next, to form a V-shaped corral (hence, my teepee nickname) with the opening facing the water. Sticks that are three feet long by two inches or so in diameter work best, and you'll have to push several support sticks into the ground perpendicular to both walls in order to prop them up. The walls should be six inches or so in height, and the set shouldn't take more than ten minutes to construct. Just keep your opening the same width as your bodygripper, place a fresh poplar stick in the back, and set your trap in the front.

My last trap had been set in an indentation the same as my first set but it was sprung with the bait stolen. This is never good. And I knew I'd have to change my strategy in order to catch this particular beaver, but being short on time, I decided to reset all four bodygrippers the same way for any less wary beavers that might still be around.

The following day all four traps were untouched with the bait stolen from each set. The beaver had shrewdly approached from the rear, managing to cop a free meal. This beaver was obviously trap shy. But beavers learn by association and can be fooled by making subtle changes to your trapping methods.

I've found that beavers will routinely enter a snare, even when it's hung in the exact same place a bodygripping trap had been the day before. Over the years, I've caught plenty of trap wise beavers with a thin loop of snare cable. But after attempting to get this particular beaver to try on a steel necklace for more than a week, I realized that I was up against an unusually timid animal.

Simple fix, I thought. Just conceal two foothold traps in front of my bait, and the beaver, after seeing a clear passage to his midnight snack, should step right into them.

I bedded two #4 coil spring traps at the entrance of my teepee set, covered both with silt, and pushed a fresh poplar stick into the ground at the back of my corral for bait. After giving the set a quick once-over, I shouldered my packbasket and headed back to my truck. The beaver would be mine by sunup I concluded cheerily. Good thing, too, because the season would end in three days, and the landowner was counting on me to save his bridge (which was taking on more water with each passing day).

Much to my dismay, I returned the following morning only to find that my bait had been stolen once again. The beaver, refusing to enter my set from the front, had deftly swiped my poplar by crawling over the back of the wooden barricade.

It's anybody's guess how the beaver knew my concealed foothold traps were waiting for him. They hadn't been sprung—hadn't even been touched. And I didn't have time to try and figure it out, either. Two more days and the season was over. I had to change my game plan so that things appeared more natural. The beaver was still attracted to my bait. This was good. All I had to do was come up with a way to make the beaver feel safe as it approached.

I scanned the opposite bank knowing I had to throw off his suspicious nature by moving to another location. There, on a gentle slope, I could see the perfect spot for my new set. Some gnarled, dead branches lying nearby would work wonders for me. I hustled over, gathered them up, and laid them along the shoreline allowing one small opening for the beaver to reach the juicy poplar sticks I'd placed several feet away. The water was shallow enough for the beaver to walk ashore, so I concealed twin Montgomery #4 coil springs side by side by the bank for a front foot catch.

I had used a burlap bag filled with rocks as a drowning weight at my previous set. It was highly visible under the water, and I thought it might have spooked the beaver. This time I anchored my drowning cable to a rusted railroad plate that would blend with the stream bottom so the beaver wouldn't notice it. I also carefully concealed my cable with mud so there would be no chance that it might alert the beaver.

I took every conceivable precaution with my new set, even making sure to lean my two poplar sticks in natural formation against the back of my tangled barrier rather than have them sticking out of the ground like they had miraculously sprouted up overnight. But when I found myself tiptoeing away after finishing the set, I had to chuckle. Apparently this shy old beaver had really gotten to me.

When I checked the traps the next morning and found them empty and the bait untouched, I figured the game was over. Ol' Chiseltooth was going to win. Somehow, he must have spotted my traps. Tomorrow was the last day of the season, and the landowner's bridge loomed in my mind. He was counting on me to save it. What would I to say to him?

I left the set as it was, hoping for a miracle, and hung two snares in well-worn beaver runs on my way back to the truck. They were my last hope. No bait, no lure, no guide sticks or fences. Just two thin strands of cable dangling in the murky water would make or break my reputation as a beaver trapper.

The following day I arrived at the pond early. The rising sun glimmered gaily off the water's surface as I stepped toward the bank. I wondered if the beautiful morning might signal good luck, when a quick side-glance toward the flooded bridge produced a wet knot in my stomach. How long before it washed away? Another quick glance at my snares confirmed what I feared most.

Both were empty.

As I trudged wearily toward my last set, I envisioned my two traps gaping back at me like two discerning eyes, waiting patiently to tell me I had failed once again.

But when I checked the set, I found two depressions in the mud where my traps had been. Although my heart pounded with anticipation, I remained cautiously optimistic. After all, the traps could be lying at the bottom of the drowning cable with only a few guard hairs pinched between their jaws. It wouldn't be the first time.

Pulling the drowning cable toward me, I could tell that something much heavier than a railroad plate was at the bottom, and I peered impatiently into the dusky water. Soon a broad, flattened tail began to materialize, quickly followed by the bulky outline of a large beaver. An immediate sense of relief washed over me. I had won. The battle was over.

But then, as the beaver surfaced, I noticed it had been caught by a hind foot. And merely by the tip of one single toe. At first I was perplexed. How could this be? I had the traps set in shallow water at the bank's edge for a front foot catch. This was a walk-in set, and the beaver certainly hadn't walked backwards into my trap!

Suddenly it dawned on me: only dumb luck had stood between my success and failure. The beaver had never come into my set after all. I hadn't fooled him one bit. Oh, he had approached all right. But he sensed that something was wrong, and as he turned his nose to my bait and kicked both hind feet down to propel himself into deep water, one foot came fatally close to a trap, and he was caught by a single toe.

I have to admit, my feelings of triumph quickly turned sour. While I was happy the landowner's bridge would be saved, a tinge of regret washed over me as I carried the beaver to my truck.

I still think about that day now and then, although it was many years ago. And at the risk of sounding a bit odd, I must confess a part of me would prefer that the beaver had never been caught at all, that instead he was still there, wreaking havoc and beckoning me to challenge him once again.

Putting the Noose on Ol' Chiseltooth

SINCE I TRAP beavers year round for nuisance control, I've had to come up with methods that are efficient under almost any conditions. I've found that snares are often my best option. They are light, compact, inexpensive, and extremely effective.

I prefer to make my own snares because I can fashion them to fit my needs under a myriad of conditions. I use 3/32" by 7x7 galvanized cable as it offers a nice loop and tremendous holding power. I also add a mid-line swivel. That way, after I make a catch, I only have to replace half the snare. The cable running from the swivel to my anchor can be used many times over.

My land snares are between six and eight feet long because beavers tend to relax more when they have room to move about. Most of my snares are equipped with treelocks. These are special ends manufactured so that snares can readily be secured to almost any sized tree. But when I can't find a suitable tree to anchor my snare, I double stake with heavy 24-inch rerod bars.

Although I've caught beaver in untreated snares, I don't recommend it. New snares should be cleaned and all shine removed. It makes them much less visible not only to the beaver but to nosy people as well. I like to simmer my snare cable in a solution of ½ cup baking soda to a gallon of water for a half hour or so and then rinse them off with tap water. This will cause the cable to take on a dull gray color and blend better with natural surroundings. I also treat my snare locks and swivels so they don't rust. A can of spray paint, flat gray or black, can treat dozens of these fittings.

I use a five-gallon plastic bucket to carry equipment on my beaver snareline. This may not be suitable if you walk long distances but most of my beaver work is done by vehicle, placing a few snares at each stop.

The bucket I use has a bungee cord wrapped around the top to hold my lure-pouch and a few small hand tools such as pliers or cable cutters stored in a separate pouch so I don't have to dig around in the pail when I need them. I put my quick-links, S-hooks, and double-stake swivels in a small metal container inside the bucket to locate them easily. Stakes, wire, hand ax, snares, and rubber gloves all fit nicely inside the bucket too. I also drill small holes into the bottom to let water drain, which helps keep my equipment dry.

Beaver snared on land at a trail set.

I rely on four different sets that have proven themselves over the years when snaring beavers. They are all blind sets. Bait or lure placed near a snare may cause the animal to slow down to investigate, so I always keep my attractors a good distance away and place my snares along travel routes leading to them. Brisk movement through the noose is what triggers the snare and ensures a solid catch.

Snares set along trails can be very productive. I try to pick a narrow spot that has a stout tree growing nearby for an anchor point, then I center my snare in the path using a 10-inch loop. I put the bottom of the snare on the ground and place a cigar-sized stepping stick across the path right up against the snare.

Often I'll take a one-inch-thick stick and split the tip open just enough to hold my cable. Pushing the stick into the ground alongside the trail, I wedge my snare cable into the split stick just behind the slide lock so the loop dangles at the trail. Next I anchor the snare end to a tree or stake it solid. It's a convenient way to secure a snare in a matter of seconds.

Dam crossovers are another excellent location to catch beavers with snares (Check state game laws when setting near beaver dams). I center my snare at the bottom of the slide and secure it the same as I do for trail sets. Beavers may not use the crossover every night, but it is a sure-fire set when they do. There is no need to conceal the snare because old chiseltooth will pay no more attention to a snare than he does to a vine in his way.

Channels created by beavers are another great location for snares. I look for narrow spots in the channel that are just wide enough for my snare. These are truly deadly sets. Wide channels can be fenced with sticks pulled from the dam, leaving an opening, or perhaps several, for your snare(s).

Deep channels are best because you don't have to contend with the beaver's feet. When a beaver walks through a snare there is always a chance that it will step directly on the cable and spring it prematurely. I like to get them swimming to eliminate this potential problem.

After creating a fence with sticks, I leave an opening bordered by forked sticks so I can drop a cross-pole into the forks. I wire my snare tightly to the cross-pole with the snare lock just touching the pole's bottom side. A loosely wired snare or support stick will cause the snare to close too slow, which could cause the beaver to back out and escape. I use a 10-inch loop (unless I'm targeting otter too, in which case a smaller loop is necessary) with the bottom two-thirds of the loop under the water because the bulk of a beaver's body is under water as it swims on the surface.

If the water current is strong, push a thin twig into the stream bottom against each side of the loop to hold your snare steady. I use peeled twigs so they are more visible and act as guide sticks for the beaver.

Occasionally I'll back away from my set and stoop low so I can see things much the same as a beaver does. This is especially useful when a snare hasn't been productive. Sometimes it helps to get down to a beaver's level in order to see what the problem is.

My favorite snare set for beavers is the dam-break set (check your game laws). It requires a little extra work but it's extremely effective and will take every beaver in a colony within a few days.

Break a 12-inch opening in a beaver dam and it will attract the first beaver out of the lodge. Additional smaller breaks, away from the main opening, will be just as attractive. A snare will guard each break, but you must not place snares directly on the dam unless you want to risk having them buried under a foot of muck when you return. I learned a long time ago that the best way to catch a beaver at a dam is to get him as he approaches the break rather than setting directly on the dam.

In order to construct the set properly, you must have the dam-break fenced off much like the channel set described above. The difference is that this fence runs in a semi-circle two feet out from the dam with a snare in its center. When the beaver swims toward the dam, he will see the opening in the fence you constructed and head straight for it. I have often set several snares like this at a single dam and found a beaver in each one the following day.

The Dam Break Set works with bodygrippers too.

Trapping Shy Beaver

THE BEAVER IS an amazing animal. In fact, our Native American Indians once referred to them as Beaver People, and it wasn't only because they watched beavers walking on their hind feet while carrying material to pack on their lodges. Imagine how impressed they must have been with an animal that was capable of building "houses" out of tree limbs and mud. Houses that resembled Indian tepees! And surely they were amazed that a simple rodent could engineer giant dams holding back thousands of tons of water.

I am just as impressed with beavers today as our Native Americans were long ago. It is truly astonishing what these animals are capable of. While most critters must adapt to environmental changes or else perish, beavers have the innate ability to change their environment to suit their specific needs. One industrious beaver can transform a wooded area that is home to deer, bear, and other upland game, into habitat suitable to fish, amphibians, and aquatic mammals in a matter of days.

And this is exactly why beavers so often wear out their welcome. I get dozens of nuisance beaver complaints every year. Farmers, landowners, and township supervisors depend on me to alleviate problems with flooding and tree damage caused by these voracious rodents. Consequently, I am compelled to remove entire beaver colonies in many instances.

Normally, the easiest way to catch beavers in open water is with bodygripping traps. Just plunk one into a beaver's run, and voila! You have your beaver.

Unfortunately, it's not always that easy.

It amazes me how a species can be so dumb that it will walk right into a 10 x 10 inch bodygripper fully exposed and sitting in a trickle of water, and then take on almost superhuman capabilities when it comes to eluding that same trap once it's been educated. There are few animals more difficult to catch than a trap-wise beaver.

Because beavers, like all animals, learn by association, sometimes the circumstances surrounding your set can alarm them as much as the trap itself. For example, if you pinch a beaver at a set using castor as an attractant, you'll likely never catch that beaver with castor again. I've even tried changing brands of commercial castor without success. One thing you *can* do, however, is make a castor mound set without any beaver castor. Just heap some mud, wet leaves, and a few peeled sticks on the bank and set your trap same as you would if you were using a lure. The scent of fresh mud alone will attract beavers, including the shy ones.

While a shy beaver may avoid castor like the plague, it's very difficult for them stay away from good bait. This is especially true after feeding under the ice for weeks or months. If their feed beds have become stale or sour, a fresh poplar branch will be very appealing to a hungry beaver. This is also true in open water if they've exhausted the poplar supply and are feeding on alternate tree types.

When switching attractants to fool shy beavers, be sure to conceal your traps as well. Your changeup in lures may bring them in, but they will avoid any exposed trap once they've been educated. And don't try to force them into your set. Fencing can be a major deterrent when trying to catch a trap wise beaver. Shy beavers do not like to be crowded. Also, keep your drowning rig concealed and make sure the captured beaver goes down deep, as far from your set as possible, so it won't be visible to the other beavers living in the colony and spook them.

Blind sets are a great way to catch shy beavers. Find where they are climbing out of the water and slip in a trap rigged for a hind foot catch. Because the trap will be set 18" deep, it won't be as noticeable and you shouldn't have to cover it.

You can also use the same idea to catch shy beavers with bait. I mentioned this set earlier but it's worth talking about it again. It is my best kept secret for taking wise beavers. Stake a 2-inch diameter poplar solidly into the bank so that the beavers can't pull it free and will have to work on it for a while. Soon they will drop their hind feet to stabilize themselves and begin to step around a bit. Your trap, or traps, preferably size four, should be 18-inches deep. Again, rig a drowning wire that sends them away from the set.

Bodygripping traps present a whole new challenge. Once a beaver decides that your bodygripper spells danger it'll never poke its head into one again unless it's skillfully concealed. They can spot these traps easily, and no matter how hard you try to hide them, Ol' Chiseltooth won't be easily fooled. Unless, of course, it's simply too late for him to react in time.

Beavers often have crossover areas on their dams. They're easy to pick out, simply look at the top of the dam and you will see a worn or discolored area leading over the dam into the water below. This pathway, or "slide" as they are often called, is caused by beavers scurrying down the dam as they travel downstream to feed. As the beavers plunge down the dam's crossover, they eventually create a hollowed area in the stream bottom where they enter the water. This area is often deep enough to completely submerge a 10 x 10 inch bodygripper.

This is a truly deadly set that will catch every beaver in the colony, including the most elusive old timers (check your state game laws regarding traps set at beaver dams). The key here is to camouflage the trap slightly so the beaver won't see it until momentum down the slide has carried him beyond the point of no return.

After completely submerging the trap, just downstream and dead center to the crossover, I place a two-inch diameter log over the trap, slightly above and in front of the jaws, to breakup the outline of the trap. I also place a peeled stick the diameter of a pencil in front of each jaw to help conceal them and act as subtle guide sticks. Next, I take a dark stick from the dam and push it between the top corner of the trap jaws and into the stream bottom at a 45-degree angle. This stabilizes the trap while simultaneously allowing it to fall free and float downstream with the beaver once I've made a catch. I also make sure the wire securing my trap is at least six feet long and place my stake downstream as well so the beaver will float far away and not alert the others.

I always place my bodygrippers upside-down when trapping beavers. You'll find that you can handle these traps much easier with the dog and trigger out of the way as you grip the jaws to submerge the trap in deep water (be careful here because the safety hooks on each spring will fall free as soon as you flip the trap over). I also bend the forked trigger at 90-degree angles like a double "L." This way the beaver has a clear, unobstructed view as he approaches the trap.

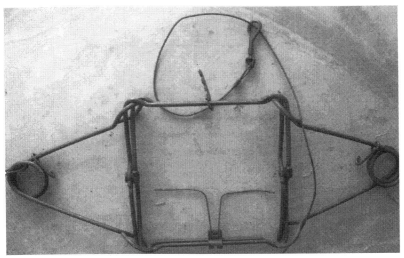

Because the beaver will be moving rapidly down the slide and on into the water, it will be into your trap before realizing it's there.

While the dam crossover set is extremely effective when trapping for shy beavers, it will also catch otters, and should never be used where these animals are protected.

This past season I was trapping a beaver lodge with bodygrippers and the first one to hit a trap happened to be a small beaver born that year. I was surprised to find the dead beaver, along with my trap, jammed under a nearby root by another member of the lodge. I suspected trouble after this and I was right. My traps were at two different entrances to the lodge, and they remained empty for several days.

I pulled them, and after trapping new territory for two weeks, returned figuring the beavers would have had time to resume normal activities and be less cautious. It was the dead of winter, and they were only moving to their feedbed and back, so I knew that the only way I'd catch them would be right at the lodge. But I also realized that they wouldn't go into my bodygripper as long as they knew it was there.

There was a lot of white pine growing nearby, so I cut two small, bushy stems and placed one in front of each entrance to the lodge. The pine needles, long and lacy, did a fine job of screening the entranceways, and I secured them so that the beavers wouldn't knock them aside when leaving the lodge. My idea was to set a bodygripper behind each pine bough but I wanted the beavers to grow used to the idea of evergreen branches just outside their entrances first. I suspected that the first time out they would slow down and be suspicious about this sudden change. If I had a trap set, they would probably detect it.

Several days later, I returned to the lodge and quietly slipped a 330 Conibear on the opposite side of each evergreen bough. The beavers had been torpedoing blindly through them on their way to their feed bed for days, and wouldn't suspect anything unusual. The evergreens did a superb job of hiding my traps, and the following morning I was rewarded with two prime pelts

Castor mound sets have been used by trappers for over two hundred years. The set is so effective it almost wiped out the entire beaver population back in the nineteenth century. Beavers mark their territory by bringing up a pile of leaves and mud from the stream bottom and depositing a yellowish secretion from their castor sacs upon it. Although foothold traps are the popular choice for this set, snares, and even bodygrippers can also be utilized.

One cold January, I was trapping an area where the beavers were traveling upstream and bulldozing their way through a foot of snow to feed on saplings in the surrounding fields. They had picked a poor location for their dam; food was scarce and their survival doubtful once winter had set in.

Due to the ice, I could only find one good spot for a snare. There was an underground spring nearby that kept the ground warm and soupy. I used my foot to scrape a fake beaver trail through a grassy opening leading to the bank, and then scooped up a basketball-sized pile of mud and leaves on the bank to imitate a castor mound. I put a gob of castor on top of the mound and set my snare in a foot of water within the grassy opening, concealing it by laying strands of dead grass over the sides and top.

The next day my snare produced a large beaver that had come after the castor so hard that it almost went completely through the snare before finally being caught around the hips. After dispatching the beaver, I spruced up the set and hung a new snare. Several more beavers were living here and I expected to have them within a few days.

But to my surprise, I found my snare empty the following morning. Other beavers had approached the set, I could see where they broke through the ice a few feet off shore, but they wouldn't come near my castor and I was sure they were spooked. Because set locations were limited, and I suspected they would avoid my snares, I decided to set a foothold trap.

I found an excellent set location nearby, but the water was relatively shallow so only a front foot catch would work. I use 1½ double coil spring traps for front foot catches on shy beavers. I know this idea may cause a few raised eyebrows, but these smaller traps are easier to conceal, and their jaw-spread is plenty wide enough for a beaver's front foot. They will hold any beaver long enough to drown and allow you to save your bigger traps for sets that actually require a wider jaw spread. You can also drown beavers in relatively shallow water with a front foot catch because they go down nose first. The only hitch is that you must be certain the beaver will be walking, not swimming, into your trap to ensure a solid front foot catch.

I used a railroad plate for a drowning weight with seven feet of cable and a one-way sliding lock. I staked the opposite end of the drowning cable into the bank and scooped a handful of mud over any exposed metal. Next I squished my foot into the muck for a trap bed and nestled my trap into the soft bottom. With only an inch of water covering my trap, I knew the beaver would be walking into the poplar stick I'd stuck into a mud pile twelve inches from the trap and slightly off center.

This is the way I catch beavers by a front foot in small traps. Whether I'm using poplar, castor, or simply a heap of mud without any attractant, my trap pan is always the width of my hand (5-inches) from the attractant, and bedded in shallow water so a beaver must walk into my bait.

The next two days produced two flat tails, and the pond was cleaned out. Although they had steered clear of my bodygripping traps and snares, I was able to fool them, as I have many others, with a carefully concealed foothold trap.

The Indentation Set

As I APPROACHED the river, I saw a fresh castor mound so large it seemed almost prehistoric. Mud and sticks had been carried to the top of a ten-foot bank and piled upon level ground in teepee fashion. The mound was several feet tall and could be seen from a considerable distance.

Here the bank dropped off steeply to the turbulent river's edge, but a portion of it was sloped enough so that I could reach the water where a small eddy had formed. There were fresh beaver tracks in the mud and the area reeked of castor. Apparently the beavers had been coming here to escape the powerful current. It was an ideal place to set traps.

There were two cuts in the bank 20 feet apart that had been created by beavers crawling out to feed in surrounding cornfields months earlier. Each indentation was just wide enough for a #330 Conibear, so I grabbed a trap from my packbasket and set it upside-down in front of the first indentation. I left most of the trap above water with the trigger submerged just under the water and bent into a double "L" so the trap offered a clear view for the beaver.

I set up the second indentation the same way, finishing the entire operation in short order. Then I climbed up the bank to admire my handiwork. There was no doubt in my mind that these sets would connect. After all, I'd been using this method for decades, taking over 100 beavers with the Indentation Set in the last several years.

But to my surprise, the next day I had a beaver caught by its hind foot in one of the Conibears and the other had been knocked completely over. At first I was baffled, but a closer inspection revealed what had happened: Apparently, after smelling the foreign castor, the beaver had scrambled wildly up the bank after the "intruder" that dared enter its territory, knocking over the first trap in its charge. Then, somehow, the beaver must have slipped backwards in the mud and jammed a hind foot into my Conibear.

Why did this happen? The only thing I could come up with is that I'd used too much castor. Good commercial beaver castor is potent stuff; too big a gob may cause a beaver to charge up the bank, sidestepping your trap as it bulldozes its way onward. Worst case scenario here is that you may have a trap shy beaver to contend with. In my case, the beaver inadvertently plunked a foot into my trap and was caught. One thing I did do right, however, was having the trap staked solidly. Always a good idea, even with "quick kill" traps, for otherwise you risk losing your trap and your catch if things go haywire like they did in this case.

I remade both sets without using beaver castor and added a fresh poplar branch for both eye appeal and drawing power. The riverbanks were devoid of any poplar, so my bait would be a tremendous enticement for any passing beaver. Its sweet aroma would also lessen the potential for another encounter with a furious flattail as it triggered the beaver's natural desire for food.

The next day I was rewarded with two fine pelts. The poplar had done its duty. Each beaver readily stuck its head into my exposed traps. I continued to catch beavers in these sets each morning until the season ended, finishing with ten prime flattails in five days.

While the Indentation Set is easy enough to construct, most waterways have cuts in the bank that are either formed by beavers or occur naturally. All you need do is locate an indentation in the bank wide enough for your bodygrip trap with enough room for your bait behind it. In the few minutes it takes to set your trap and place your bait, you'll have one of the best beaver producers ever seen on any trapline.

Poplar bait stick is behind trap. Support stick through jaws

Triple Play Trapline

THE QUARRYMAN WAS GRATEFUL to see me but adamant about the beavers invading his property. He wanted every one of them removed. They had been raising water levels all summer long, and he'd grown weary of tearing out dams only to find them repaired overnight.

There were several small abandoned quarries on the property, each separated by narrow haul roads. Underground springs had filled the quarries with water and the surrounding landscape was dotted with poplar trees. Although the pesky rodents had been visiting each of the ponds, they had set up shop in the main quarry, which was about five acres in size. Two big lodges rested on a thin strip of land intersecting the quarry, and hundreds of poplar trees had been gnawed down along its outer rim.

It was late February, the ice still thick and covered with snow, but there was one open patch of water the size of a child's bedroom in the pond. Fortunately, it was just off the roadway, and fresh beaver tracks could be seen along the snow-covered bank.

I was certain that every beaver in the pond shared this small open area. They had been locked under the ice, living in a world of darkness for months. Their feedbeds had grown sour in that time. Surely the lure of open water and fresh, clean air would appeal to them. And I was certain that a poplar branch protruding from the sunny and glistening bank would be a fatal attraction to every beaver in the pond.

I grabbed a bundle of three-foot-long beaver sticks from the bed of my truck and staked out a U-shaped fence that ran from the bank into shallow water where I left an opening for my trap. The sticks were spaced two inches apart and formed a pen about 18 inches long. After peeling a section of green bark from a poplar branch, I stuck it into the bank at the rear of the pen and set a size 330 Conibear in the water at the opposite end. By peeling fresh bark from the bait stick, I added eye appeal and enhanced the poplar's aroma, making my set all the more attractive.

Searching for another set location, I spotted a double run coming from under the ice into the open water surrounding me. The run split, forming a Y around a dry sandbar littered with stumps of rotted wood.

It looked like a perfect spot for two bodygrippers, so I lowered a Conibear into one of the runs until it hit bottom. The trap filled the run perfectly from side to side but the top jaws were even with the water surface and had to be moved up. With jaws set close to the surface, a beaver is more apt to knock the trap down or spring it as they try to push themselves over the jaws.

I raised the trap and wedged the left spring into a tangle of roots bordering the run to stabilize it. Then I pushed the opposite spring into the soft sand at the bottom. This brought the top of the trap two inches above the water line.

After setting the second bodygripper in the other run, I used a five-foot poplar limb for bait, pushing it into the bottom, back from the traps, with several feet protruding above the water for eye appeal. In this case, I wanted the beavers to approach my bait while swimming on the surface (When I want a beaver to approach under water, I completely submerge my bait stick).

The following morning each trap held beavers. Although they were close to the road, I had to negotiate a very steep and slippery bank to haul them out. Fortunately, I had a pair of beaver handles to help me carry the cumbersome critters back to my truck. A long-time friend, Tom Scarpello, gave me a set several years ago, and I've never been without them since.

Beaver handles are easy to make. Start by taking a one-inch thick dowel and cut two pieces, six inches long. Drill a hole ¾-inches from each end just big enough for your snare cable to slide through. Next, cut four 13-inch lengths of cable (two for each handle), hammer an aluminum ferrule on each end and add a washer before slipping the opposite ends though each hole. Now slide a double ferrule onto the free end of each cable and form a loop by inserting the cable back through the double-holed ferrule. Finish by hammering a single ferrule on the cable end and your double ferrule becomes a slipknot for a convenient, running noose.

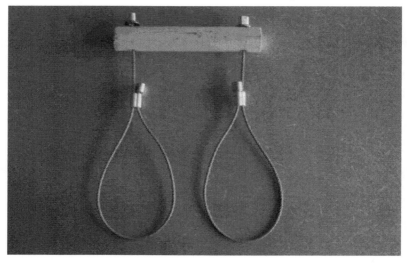

When you want to transport a beaver, cinch one loop over a hind foot, the other over a front foot and pick the beaver up with your handle. Now you can easily carry one of the hefty critters in each hand and they won't slip through your grip.

As it turned out, that tiny section of open water attracted every beaver in the pond, and my fresh poplar bait brought them charging into my traps. I ended up catching three each day for three days straight. A triple of triples so to speak.

I often find pinpoint locations on my traplines that are visited by large numbers of furbearers. In this case, the harsh winter conditions made a small patch of open water appeal to an entire beaver colony. Rich fur pockets can be found on every trapline if you take the time to look for them.

The Leaning Post Set

THIS SET WAS DESCRIBED to me by a friend, Barry Warner, who was trapping a swampy area for beavers where set locations were few and far between. He and his partner had agreements with several landowners to do some serious damage control on the beaver population, but the soggy terrain was hampering their best efforts. Oh, they were catching beavers all right, and plenty of them, but they had to spend too much time finding suitable trap locations in the deep and murky waters.

One day Barry was standing along a beaver dam when he noticed two trees growing in the water that happened to be about a snare-width apart. Why not place a snare between the twin trees along with a dab of his favorite lure, he thought. The beaver would circle the trees in an attempt to locate the bait, eventually working its way between them and into his snare. Barry waded out and secured a snare, then smeared a nice gob of attractant on the bark about 18-inches above it. The following morning he was rewarded with a dandy flattail.

Although this set has its limitations because twin trees standing one snare-loop apart are required to make it work, trappers can employ the same idea with the Leaning Post Set.

The set is simple and takes only a few minutes to complete. Begin by searching for a tree that is standing in water near the beaver's travel way. Next, lean a two or three-inch diameter post against the tree (or other suitable backstop, like a steep bank) in an angle to create a narrow opening for the beaver to pass between the post and the tree. Make sure the bottom of your post has been pushed into the mud only enough to support your snare. Hang the snare off the tree centered in the opening you've created and secure the end to the tree, well under water, especially if the tree has a small diameter. That way, if a beaver chews through the tree it won't swim off with your snare. Since the beaver will approach your snare while swimming on the surface, the snare should have a 10-inch loop with about 1/3 of the loop above water.

Next, place some beaver castor or your favorite lure on the post about a foot or so above the snare. You want to keep the lure relatively high so the beaver won't be able to pinpoint where it's coming from.

Do not secure your post to the tree or jam it too tightly into the mud. One of the trick ideas about this set is for the captured beaver to eventually knock the post into the water after it gets tangled in your snare. This lessens the chance that other beavers will associate the smell of your attractant with their captured mate.

The Leaning Post set will also work with bodygripping traps. When using bodygrippers you'll have to find a location where the water depth allows two or three inches of the trap above water or find a large rock or other platform to support the trap in order to keep the top jaw above the waterline.

Often I'll overhear a trapper complaining about a particular beaver that continues to elude his traps, knowing all the while that leaning post set, along with a well-placed snare and a change-up in attractant, would most likely solve the problem.

Steering Mink into your Traps

SINCE THE KEY TO successful trapping is location, if you can look at a stream and pick out areas where mink will likely travel, you'll be well on your way to a productive trapline. With this in mind, it's important to know that although they are expert swimmers, mink spend most of their time running along the bank rather than gliding through water like muskrats, beavers, and otters do.

Many trappers realize that mink frequent places like tree roots pictured below that border stream banks. Blind sets are usually made at these locations simply by pressing a trap against the edge of the bank and walking away. Thousands of mink have been caught this way, and thousands more missed.

Because mink like to squeeze into narrow passageways, you would increase your catch dramatically by squaring off these protruding tree roots with flat-sided rocks as seen below. These stone pillars narrow down the mink's pathway while simultaneously creating an enchanting tunnel that will be difficult for any curious mink to pass up (note jump stick).

Another unique behavioral characteristic of mink is that they like to hug close to perpendicular walls. Perhaps this trait comes from their susceptibility to avian predation. Trappers can take advantage of this knowledge by using a spade to straighten a section of stream bank where mink are known to travel. By creating a perpendicular wall, you will force any passing mink to walk directly into your trap, which should be set in one inch of water with one jaw tight against the bank.

I often place a jump stick about the size of a pencil just ahead of my trap. Mink move fast. A jump stick slows them down and may increase your catch.

Be sure to set traps along bridge walls in the same fashion. Bridge abutments are deadly locations for mink. And if the water is too deep, simply cut a piece of sod and place it grass-side-down along the bridge wall so that your trap will be under approximately an inch of water when resting on the sod.

Lures don't seem to work well on mink. A good gland lure might keep them nosing around your set for a spell, but I've never seen a lure pull a mink for any great distance, which is why pinpoint location and sets with eye appeal are so important when trapping these valuable furbearers.

Blind sets like those described above are good, but nothing beats the pocket set when trapping mink. Pocket sets have tremendous drawing power and can be made almost anywhere a mink might travel. They also save you the time of searching for that perfect blind set. In other words, a good pocket set will make the mink come to you, and it might even cross a stream to get to it, provided you make the set with plenty of eye appeal. Placed strategically, pocket sets give the trapper a triple advantage because they combine the visual attraction of a hole in the bank and the alluring aroma of fresh bait to a well-chosen set location.

When trapping mink, I look for a bank with a moderate slope and dig a six-inch wide hole on a slight upward angle until it's a foot deep. This angle allows water to run several inches into the hole to cover my trap while the remaining portion provides a dry shelf to pin my bait.

A sloping bank is better than a vertical one because you can form a channel leading into your hole. This channel, or knee wall so to speak, helps guide the mink directly into your trap, and it should be just wide enough to bed your trap with each jaw touching its sides. Because some mink will only peek into the hole rather than enter it, I'm careful to set my traps just outside the entrance.

Muskrats make great mink bait, and I quarter my 'rat carcasses after skinning them for future use on my mink line. A good-sized hunk of fresh muskrat wrapped in a wad of grass will get a passing mink to at least steal a glance into your pocket set, even if he does have a full belly. Covering your bait with grass adds to its allure and causes the mink to spend more time investigating your set, thereby improving your chances of making a catch.

After bedding my trap solidly so there is no wobble to spook the mink, I smear up the bank around my set until it glistens. This helps to add visibility to the set, making it more attractive to any passing mink.

Pocket sets can be made almost anywhere, but some of the best locations are near bridge abutments and road culverts because these are natural funnels for mink. Overhanging root formations and undercut banks are also great places to make pocket sets. Although mink normally check out these areas, and blind sets routinely take them here, the addition of a baited pocket set will increase your chances of steering these sleek, super predators directly into your trap.

Make Muskrats Come to You

AFTER DRIVING PAST the pond the first time, I quickly turned around, hoping to set some traps. Acres of lush green grass surrounded its banks, making it ideal for muskrats.

As I drove into the property, a farmer stepped out from the barn to greet me, so I asked for permission to trap muskrats.

"Sure!" he replied cheerily. He hooked two meaty thumbs into his suspenders. "Nobody's trapped here in years, and I see muskrats swimming around all the time. Help yourself."

"Where do you see them?" I asked.

"Come on," he motioned with a wave of his hand. "Follow me."

I ambled over to the pond with my new friend and soon found myself staring into the dark water below. There was a three-foot-wide culvert pipe submerged beneath our feet. Behind us, a warm spring ran under a farm road and emptied into the culvert at the other end.

The farmer pointed to a jumble of heavy rocks deep under the water at the bottom of the culvert. "See that opening between those rocks?" he said. "That's where the muskrats go."

I would never have considered setting a trap there if the farmer hadn't told me about it. The pond's bottom was hardpan; there were no tracks or tail-drag marks to indicate that muskrats were using the tiny opening.

The gap between the rocks was big enough for a muskrat to squeeze through, but too narrow to accommodate a bodygripper, so after grabbing my hip boots, I stepped into the frigid water and gently separated the rocks just wide enough to snuggle a 110 Conibear between them.

"Pretty slick," beamed the farmer. "Think you could catch the mink that's been killing my chickens, too? I watched him run into the culvert at the opposite end."

Happy to oblige, I leaned a flat rock against the opening to narrow it down and set two number one Stoploss traps in shallow water, one on each side, tight to the wall.

From there I walked back to the pond, looking to set a few more traps. But there were so many trails coming up the bank I would have needed dozens of foothold traps to cover them all.

It was frustrating. The pond was obviously loaded with 'rats but the water was too dark to see their den entrances. I tried walking along while prodding the bank with my foot, but the rocky bottom was covered with a slippery silt that made navigation extremely difficult. Rather than risk a cold bath or some broken bones, I decided to move on to new territory until I could come up with a way to trap the pond.

But as it turned out, I didn't have to figure out a thing. My mink set caught three mink in three consecutive days, and my Conibear set between the two rocks caught 14 muskrats in the following weeks.

I continue to set traps at the farm pond every year using the same sets. I usually take a mink or two at the warm spring and the rock gap produces quite a few 'rats each season. Because the farm is near a big marsh, which is off limits to trapping, muskrats are continually moving into the pond, and I never have to worry about over harvesting the population.

When trapping farm ponds, I often find a single location that is frequented by most or all of the muskrats living there. These hot spots save me a lot of time because I don't have to spend hours setting up every den or run on my trapline in order to make a good catch. While it may take longer to harvest a dozen muskrats this way, it still works out well for me as long as I'm passing the area anyway, on my way to check other traps.

I had a similar incident that produced surprising results on my muskrat trapline this year. I was trapping a farm pond that was 50-percent marsh. There was a half-inch of ice blanketing the mucky bottom close to shore, consequently, it wouldn't hold me, and with each step I took, my foot broke through the ice and plunged into the sucking mud below. But because of the numerous feed beds and chewed roots I found, I decided to slog onward.

Three muskrat houses were nestled among cattails in the back of the pond, and while making my way toward them I noticed a patch of cloudy water under the ice below me. There was no bank here. The landscape simply rolled into the water in a gradual slope, typical of any marsh. On a whim, I stomped through the ice and suddenly found my boot sliding into a perfect den hole hidden fifteen inches below the grassy surface. I wouldn't have found it had it not been for the cloudy water indicating activity under the ice, and I quickly set a bodygripper at the hole and moved on.

After reaching the muskrat houses, I was both disappointed and surprised to see that each had been abandoned. I hadn't brought any foothold traps with me for the feed beds I'd seen, and travel was so arduous that I decided to leave with only my single bodygripping trap at the hole I had found.

On my way back to my truck, I heard some splashing and saw that a muskrat had just been caught in my trap. After collecting the 'rat, I reset my trap and moved on, making a mental note that the muskrat had been going into the hole, not coming out, when it was caught.

The following day I had another muskrat in my trap. It too had been caught entering the hole. Turns out that this was some kind of gathering spot for the muskrats in the pond. I caught five more 'rats in as many days, and each one had been attempting to enter the hole I'd found.

Because the season ended, I don't know how many more muskrats could have been using the it. However, I flagged the hole with a tall wooden stake so I can catch muskrats here for many years to come, even if it's buried under heavy snow and ice before I get there.

One thing I've learned over the years is to always ask the landowner where he sees furbearers on his property. No one is more intimate with the surrounding landscape than a person who lives and works on his own land. They can often tell you where animals travel and help you calculate how many furbearers to expect in a given area.

But no matter whether you luck into a hotspot as I did in the marsh, or find one by checking with the landowner, hot spots can be found at almost every waterway on your trapline. And once they're located, you can make the muskrats come to you for many seasons to come.

Streamlined Muskrat Trapping

ALTHOUGH IT'S BEEN decades since I caught my first muskrat, I'll never forget the thrill of that day. Blood coursed through my veins at light-speed. The muskrat was alive, caught by a hind foot along a shallow stream, its dark fur glistened in the morning sun.

I was hooked on trapping from that moment on, especially muskrat trapping. There is something about catching these brown jewels of the waterways that brings a smile to my face to this day. I guess you have to be a trapper to understand.

My early sets were simple affairs. Bodygrippers plugged in front of underwater dens and footholds set along well-worn trails. Nothing fancy. Just run a wire off the chain ring and stake it into deep water. A number one longspring was heavy enough to drown the muskrat, especially if it found something in the water to tangle up in.

Thing is, I don't set traps much differently today. Oh, I've learned a few tricks over the years that have helped streamline my 'rat trapping. And I'll share them with you in a moment. But for the most part, the key to successful muskrat trapping is simple, basic techniques.

Den sets are the most productive method for catching muskrats, but it can be difficult to locate them at times. I remember one pond, years ago, so muddy it was like setting traps in pea soup. There was plenty of muskrat sign along the banks, but it would have been impractical to cover every trail, so I began wading blindly along the water in hip boots while prodding the bank with my toe. One by one, I found every den. They were deep, almost over the top of my boots, and I had to set them by feel.

The method I used was simple. Once my foot slid into a suspected den entrance I inched my foot backwards until my boot was halfway out of the hole. From there I took a number 110 bodygripping trap, and while holding it by the chain, lowered the trap until it touched the top of my boot. Then I backed my foot completely out of the hole, which enabled me to settle the trap directly in front of the den entrance with the spring pointing up.

I took a two-foot-long beaver stick and slid it through the spring's end ring by feel, lightly tapping up and down inside the ring with the end of my stick to be sure I got it right. The trick was to slide the stake through the ring in a 45-degree angle so that it pushed down on the spring. This provided pressure on my trap and kept it secure against the bottom. I also pressed the trap's perpendicular spring against the bank above the den entrance for additional stability.

When muskrats leave the den, their momentum tends to propel them into the trap, and as long as your stake is narrower than the spring ring, the trap will swivel on the stake. This setup allows captured muskrats to float up from the den entrance, out of the way for the next one to leave the den. This way I can set multiple traps along a run leading into the den. The muskrats are easier to find, too, especially in murky water.

Eventually I had ten bodygrippers set at separate den entrances. The next day they produced eight nice 'rats. The landowner had asked me to remove all the muskrats, and I was able to accomplish this in three days with my ten sets. Had I not taken the initiative to search diligently for dens, I would have been there for a week or more checking dozens of traps due to the terrific abundance of sign. By setting up dens only, I was able to use more of my limited time to work other complaint areas and add to my season's tally of fur.

But sometimes you simply cannot find any dens, and must resort to other methods. In this case, I set foothold traps along muskrat trails heavily covered with fresh tracks. When possible I will also use bodygrippers on 'rat trails. Toilet areas piled high with dung are another likely place to catch muskrats if dens are scarce.

Muskrats are creatures of habit, just like we humans. If you catch one muskrat in a specific location, you're likely to catch more. When dens are difficult to find, look for underwater runs, large feed beds, and travel routes that lead to other waterways. Most small farm ponds will have at least one location visited by virtually every muskrat. Sometimes it will be a feed den or a culvert or spring leading from the pond to another waterway. These locations are deadly, and a trapper can clean out an entire muskrat population with one trap, checked daily, over time.

Muskrats are not difficult to drown provided there is nothing for them to tangle on along the bank first. If they do, and it's a front foot catch, they'll quickly snap their tiny wrist, enabling them to wring out of a trap in seconds.

As stated earlier, many of the farm ponds on my trapline have community den sites that make it possible to harvest an entire muskrat population over a short period of time. One such location could be found at the next pond I visited. The den hole was deep with a long, broad run leading into it. And because the run was wide, I needed to narrow things down a bit so the frisky little rodents would swim directly into my bodygripper as they torpedoed along.

I took a Conibear from my trap bucket and centered it on the bottom of the run, just in front of the den hole, with its spring sticking straight up. Next, I eased two of my beaver sticks through the eye of the spring in crisscross fashion, being careful to run them just outside the trap's jaws as I pushed them into the mud to secure my trap. The two stakes formed an X, with the bottom half serving as guide posts while the top half encouraged the muskrat (or mink) to stay low because the perpendicular spring, along with the crossed sticks, form a barrier. If your bodygripping trap has a chain attached, simply loop it around one of the upper sticks so it will be out of the way.

Next, I set two additional Conibears along the run exactly the same way. The three traps were placed 18" apart to prevent a captured muskrat from tangling in the next trap. The nice thing about this setup is that the crossed stakes hold your trap steady and serve as guideposts while still allowing the captured muskrat to float up and out of the way for a clear path to the next trap. Just be sure to use sticks about the size of your index finger so they won't bind the spring eye and prevent your trap from swiveling.

The three sets took only a few minutes to complete, and I was about to leave when I noticed what looked like another den hole under some green vegetation in the bank. I took a long step over my traps and stuffed a foot into the hole. It went back a few inches and stopped dead. Apparently, muskrats had been digging for roots but had long since abandoned the project.

I often find old holes like this on my trapline and they make great places to set traps. All you need do is freshen things up a bit and be you'll amazed at how often muskrats will revisit these holes. This particular one was close to the surface so I slicked up the bank for eye appeal and reamed out the hole with my foot until it was five inches deep and just wide enough for my bodygripper.

The following morning, all four traps held muskrats—a double on doubles, so to speak. I always set my bodygripping traps with the dog (trigger latch) facing away from the den hole. That way, after a catch is made, I can tell whether I have muskrats living inside or if it's being frequented by outsiders, making it what I call a community den. With my three traps at the den, one 'rat was caught exiting while the other two Conibears held muskrats heading into the den.

My Conibear at the hole I'd freshened with my foot had lured a curious muskrat as well. But I wasn't too surprised, as I often catch them this way. In fact, it doesn't matter whether the hole is near the surface or down deep, either way you can catch muskrats by sprucing up old forage holes with your foot. When they're deep, I use my heel to gouge a fresh run through the stream bottom that leads to the hole. This adds eye appeal and encourages passing muskrats to take a fatal peek. It's an especially good way to snag extra fur when good set locations are scarce but muskrats plentiful.

I retrieved my Conibear with the muskrat still inside and grasped it firmly by the jaws next to the spring. Then I snapped my wrists in short, rapid strokes. This shakes the water off my muskrat like a dog coming in from the rain. Just be sure to turn your face so you don't get caught in the spray (snow is even better, just roll the muskrat—or any wet critter—through the white powder and the pelt will fluff like it just came out of a clothes dryer).

After shaking all four muskrats dry in the same manner, I wrapped them in newspaper to soak up any remaining damp spots and placed them in my truck. It was the beginning of a great day, and I was looking forward to checking the rest of my traps.

Rock Solid Bodygrippers

TRAPPING IN NORTHEASTERN Pennsylvania can be difficult due to the rocky terrain that trappers are forced to deal with. Often, it is nearly impossible to pound a stake into the ground. This is especially true with water trapping, where many of our streambeds are granite hard and lined by rocky outcroppings.

I began using rocks to stabilize bodygrippers many years ago when trapping beaver along a rocky streambed. A landowner had contacted me the day before beaver season ended and asked me if I could clean out the entire colony.

Due to the thin ice around the dam, I found few suitable trap locations. But I did notice that the beavers were walking up and down the shallow streambed above the dam. Throwing caution to the wind, I decided to stick a number of bodygrippers in the center of the creek where the beavers were moving upstream for food.

Of course, it was impossible to stake my traps, so I simply set them in the center of the two-inch-deep streambed with their springs extending straight out like the wings on an airplane. I filled the space under each spring with a large flat rock and placed another heavy rock on top, sandwiching them (it isn't always necessary to brace both springs when supporting bodygrippers). The rocks not only stabilized my traps but also served as stone columns for the beaver to pass through.

The following morning my experiment paid off better than I had ever dreamed. Each trap held a prime beaver. They had walked unafraid, right into my exposed bodygrippers.

While trapping muskrats and mink in rocky streams, I also come across good set locations where it's impossible to stake my trap solid. After all, the trap must be held firmly in place as the animal passes through the jaws, and most of us are used to simply running a stake through the trap springs or between the jaws and into the ground to accomplish this. But when setting traps along rocky streams, we often have to resort to alternative methods.

While bodygripping traps can be stabilized quickly and efficiently using rocks, we also need to anchor the trap to something. To remedy this, I either wire my trap chain to a heavy rock or center a wooden stake through the chain ring and lay it on the ground with a good-sized rock on top of the stake. The wooden stake helps the rocks bite down on the chain ring and keeps it from slipping off the stake. A properly sized and adjusted bodygripper in good condition will kill a muskrat or mink quickly, so it's not necessary to anchor it as firmly as a foothold trap.

I have two favorite spots to trap muskrats in a farm pond near my home. The pond has lots of muskrats but the water is dark and the rocks are covered with silt, and extremely slippery. Walking in the pond, attempting to find muskrat dens by prodding with my boots, proved comical. I spent most of the time with my arms flailing about like a drunken tightrope walker. So rather than risk injury, I decided to set traps at two primary places: a warm spring that ran under a rocky culvert into the pond, and a feedbed underneath a wooden boat dock.

The warm spring was only a few inches deep where it first entered the culvert, which was hemmed by large rocks. I used a flat rock to block off most of the opening, leaving just enough space to squeeze a 110 bodygripper between my rock and the culvert's stone wall. The bodygripper was set hinge-side-down, with the spring extending into the air. My inserted rock holds the trap against the culvert wall and it's ready to fire. Often I can find a rock that will slide partially inside the open trap jaws, stabilizing it even more by preventing trap wobble. As long as the trap's dog isn't obstructed, the trap will work fine.

Rocky culvert before

Rocky culvert after

The boat dock held plenty of muskrat sign along the muddy bank that ran under it, so I blocked off the opening with rocks leaving just enough space to wedge a bodygripper between two of the rocks. I ran the trap chain up to an old nail that jutted conveniently above and hooked one of the links onto it. The set only took a few minutes to complete, and I caught several muskrats with it that season. I continue to catch a goodly number of muskrats there each year, ever since. So, the next time you break into a cold sweat as you try to ram a stake through the ground at that perfect set location, put down that hammer, step back, and look around. There may be a way to make a rock solid set after all.

Note flat rock above on right is tucked just inside trap jaws

Guarding Your Catch

I STILL HAVE SEVERAL dozen number one Victor Stoploss traps that I acquired as a schoolboy trapper. I use these traps almost exclusively when setting footholds for muskrats, although I own more than 300 traps.

The number one Victor Stoploss and similar sized guard traps have many advantages over conventional longsprings and jumps. Their chief asset being a guarantee, almost to an absolute certainty, that your catch will be there when you check your trap. I've never lost a muskrat or mink that had stepped into one of these traps, and I've caught my fair share over the years.

But I would be remiss if I didn't say that the same does not hold true for the number 1½ Stoploss trap. I purchased a half-dozen some years ago at what I thought was a bargain price. After setting them, I was surprised to find that several muskrats had managed to wring off a front foot on my first morning's check. These traps are too big and powerful for 'rats and I've never used them since.

But the number one Stoploss, especially the longspring, is the perfect trap for muskrats and mink. It will hold raccoons when they stumble into them too. However, I try to keep them out of these traps because they fight hard and tend to ruin the guard bar. If I think there is a chance that I might catch a raccoon, I attach several additional feet of chain and a grapple or drag to my trap.

My Stoploss traps are rigged with two feet of chain and two universal swivels, one in the middle and another at the end. This way I can run a rerod stake through the swivel in the center of the chain when I want to keep the stake close for den sets, or stake in deep water when conditions are right. When using Stoploss traps in shallow water I'll often stake the trap so the muskrat can crawl several inches back into its den entrance and hide. A muskrat visible on the bank, dead or alive, is likely to be found by dogs, raccoons, a passing mink or any number of avian predators. Trap thieves might also be attracted to the sight of a muskrat or mink high and dry along a stream bank. Also, keep in mind that guard traps restrict the movement of your catch, and will often cause a muskrat or mink to drown in shallow water.

Stoploss traps rigged with center and end swivels

Occasionally I run across a perfect place to set a trap knowing my catch will have to remain above water in order to make the set work. With guard traps, you don't have to worry about your muskrat footing out. Even a toe catch will likely be there for you when you check your line. I've often found muskrats dead in my Stoploss traps when caught by a front foot after being struck in the head by the guard bar.

All guard type traps have a pin attached to the chain that slips between the guard bar and trap spring preventing the bar from triggering until the trap jaws close. When an animal is caught, it jerks the chain taught which pulls out the pin allowing the guard bar to close over your catch. Therefore, it's important to double check that you haven't inadvertently pulled the pin free from the guard bar while completing your set. Results are often an empty trap. The guard bar can act as a catapult, helping to propel your catch out of the trap, if it fires simultaneously with the jaws.

When possible, I use window sash weights to anchor my Stoploss traps when setting in rocky streambeds. Mine date back to the 1920s, and were used to counterbalance the load of closed windows, allowing them to be opened more easily. Made of iron, they come in various sizes and weights. I find them by scavenging around old, demolished buildings. I've occasionally seen them at yard sales, too. All window sash weights have a hole at one end so a cord could be tied to them for operation inside a window frame. This makes them ideal as drags or drowning weights on the trapline.

When setting traps for mink along bridge walls like I did above, the window weight can serve a duel purpose. Not only does it make a handy anchor for your trap, it can also help you catch more mink. I use a weight that is one inch thick and lay it just in front of my trap, which is nestled tight against the bridge wall. When a mink comes scampering along at light speed it will slow down as it approaches the weight, only to jump over it directly into my trap.

I leave window my sash weights at key set locations all year long so I can come back and reset later in the season. I use heavy wire or a quick link to secure the weight to my trap, and in seconds I'm ready to move on to my next set.

Trap attached to window sash weight with quick link

Guard type traps are an asset to the trapline. If you're looking to add some steel to your collection, you might want to consider a dozen or two. At approximately one dollar extra in cost per trap, they will pay for themselves many times over. Window sash weights are a better deal yet. Usually a few bucks will buy all you can carry back to your vehicle.

The Invisible Bait Set

PENNSYLVANIA'S MINK AND muskrat season had opened 24 hours ago, and I found myself busily putting up my morning's catch of 10 plump 'rats. The carcasses were dropped one by one into a plastic bucket as I skinned them.

After putting the hides on steel fur forms and hanging them to dry, I cut each muskrat carcass into halves for mink bait. Most of 'rats were stored in my freezer for future use, but I did keep several in the bucket for the day's trapline. Although I only had time to make a dozen sets, the sun was shining and the better part of a mild November afternoon awaited me.

Although many baits and lures have been known to attract mink, I have found fresh muskrats to be irresistible to them. And judging by the number of mink that blunder into traps at muskrat den entrances, this voracious super-predator must be hunting them at every opportunity.

My first set of the day was at a stone bridge abutment along a stream. There is a 3-inch wide fissure in a support column near the water line where I've caught mink each season for a number of years. I took a muskrat half from my bucket and stuffed it inside the crack, then I scooped out a bed for my trap and placed a 1-½ double coil spring in front of the bait. No other scent or lure was needed. Any mink that used the bridge was sure to pick up the tantalizing aroma.

I continued up stream and made another set for mink along an eddy. The bank showed plenty of mink tracks, and it looked perfect for a pocket set. I dug a deep hole that sloped slightly uphill and stuffed half a muskrat inside. Nestling a double coil spring into the soft mud in front of the hole, I tossed the chain and grapple into deep water and wedged a jump stick in front of the trap.

After setting all the traps but one, I was about to head back for my truck when I noticed an overhanging bank that looked perfect for a mink set. Unfortunately, my carcass bucket was already empty. No matter, I thought. The bank looked too good to pass up; I had one more trap and decided to make a blind set.

After finishing, I reached for my empty bucket and was about to leave when the idea hit me like a freight train: There were tiny bits of muscle tissue smeared inside the bucket, and a puddle of blood and body fluids covered the bottom. The plastic pail absolutely reeked of muskrat. I dipped it into the stream and sloshed the water around until it turned pink. Then I pitched the water on the bank above my trap so it ran down into the stream. The soft earth became saturated with the aroma of fresh muskrat; hence, my Invisible Bait Set was born.

The following day I had a large buck mink in my trap at the overhanging bank and a nice female at the bridge. The mink caught in my Invisible Bait Set delighted me. I was certain that it was no fluke. That mink didn't just happen by; it was pulled to the bank by the strong scent of muskrat. I've used the set many times since that day, and have found it to be a consistent producer.

I realize that the Invisible Bait Set has its limitations, and can't be used with the same regularity as conventional bait sets, but it does have its place, and it has some advantages over solid muskrat baits.

The overhanging bank is a prime example. Mink love to investigate these areas, but if your trap isn't placed just right, the mink may miss it. Bait keeps the mink at your set and increases your chances of making a catch. By using the Invisible Bait Set, it's just like staking a giant muskrat carcass next to your trap. The big difference is that the bait is not visible.

The muskrat smell emanating from the bank should last several days to a week in mild, dry weather and will keep any passing mink running back and forth as it attempts to locate its prey, eventually passing over your trap. In fact, it's often a good idea to place more than one trap at the same location when using this set because the bait is always working for you. It can't be stolen. And what's more, no self-respecting mink in its right mind will pass it up.

Efficient Raccoon Trapping

THE RACCOON CAN provide a generous added profit to your trapline because they are usually found in good numbers and aren't difficult to lure into a trap. Prices seem to be going up too. So now is a great time to think about adding a few more raccoon sets to your trapline.

You don't always have to trap near water to take large numbers of raccoons. During autumn months, raccoons are still working cornfields heavily, and they will continue to make regular trips into grain fields throughout the winter like the one pictured below.

Wooded areas, even when the nearest stream is a considerable distance, are also great places to find raccoons because they'll be gorging themselves on fruits and nuts in preparation for the winter months.

Look for their toilet areas at the base of large trees, especially those that have fallen. Some of these areas will be piled high with dung. Examine the droppings carefully to see what they have been feeding on; usually it'll be corn or wild berries. Be sure to set up these locations, particularly if the dung appears fresh. You're certain to catch a sizeable number of raccoons, and don't be surprised if you snag a gray fox or two as well.

Of course, you don't want to pass up the streams and ponds along the way. Road culverts, bridges, and tributaries leading into larger waterways are natural funnels for raccoons. Traps set in these locations can reap huge benefits. Be sure to gang trap any area that serves as a bottleneck for raccoons. They are social animals, and you'll often score doubles if you have the traps ready.

Baited dirtholes and pocket sets will catch raccoons quickly and require little effort. The most attractive baits for raccoons contain fish or sweet smelling scents. Shellfish oil, fruit paste baits, and even canned cat food work well. If you're trapping muskrats, quarter the carcasses and you'll have one of the best raccoon baits you can find.

Be sure to dig your dirtholes and pocket sets eight to ten inches deep so the raccoon can't steal your bait. These rascals have front feet much like hands and will often reach into holes and pull out the bait when possible. Keep your pocket sets along stream banks six inches wide. A wider pocket presents a visual attraction to any furbearer, especially the ever-curious raccoon.

When targeting raccoons along stream banks, I set my trap back about eight inches and offset it from the hole for a hind foot catch, which is best unless you use a drowning rig. A raccoon's hind foot is much heavier than its slim front foot and will not be damaged so long as your traps aren't oversized. One caution with hind foot catches: when using stakes, be certain to eliminate anything that the raccoon can grab with its front paws to help it pull out of your trap.

The number 1-½ double coilspring is preferred by most trappers for general all around use. This is the trap I've used to catch most of my raccoons over the years. Some trappers also use the number 11 double longspring. I've even heard of a few who claim good success using the number one single longspring for raccoons.

Regardless of what trap you prefer, it will usually have to be adjusted if purchased new. I file any round edges from the dog and adjust the pan so it sets level with or just below the jaws when set. This goes for all furbearers, not just raccoons. Aside from this, be sure that your trap rests solid in its bed. Raccoons are curious animals. If they place a foot on a jaw before hitting the pan and feel movement, your trap is sure to be toyed with. This usually results in a sprung trap, or worse, a toe catch. You will rarely hold a raccoon caught by its toes unless you drown it or happen to check the trap soon after it's caught.

The raccoon has long feet, and if part of its foot rests on the jaw at the same time it steps on the pan, the closing jaws may throw its foot clear or result in a toe catch. You can minimize this problem by placing the trap so the raccoon steps between the jaws rather than over them or by using a stepping stick to guide its foot directly to the trap pan.

The most difficult part of raccoon trapping is holding the animal after it's caught. Drowning sets are a good idea when possible, but a lack of deep water, coupled with time restraints, can make drowning rigs out of the question for many trappers. If you must stake your trap, use swivels to prevent the trap from tangling with ground debris as the raccoon (or any animal, for that matter) struggles. If your trap doesn't swivel freely it will damage the animal's foot, which may aid in a pull out. Also, keep your trap chain at six inches to prevent the animal from taking strong lunges that could dislodge its foot.

When trapping raccoons, I use weighted drags or coyote grapples with six feet of chain whenever possible. I always secure one double swivel at the base of the trap, another at the chain's center, and one more where it attaches to the grapple. One big advantage to this rig is that the raccoon will tangle in the brush rather than be held solidly to a stake, which makes it extremely difficult to pull out of a trap. Your catch is also more inclined to fight the surrounding brush that has him tangled rather than the trap itself, which keeps him from injuring his foot.

Raccoon tangled in grapple and chain

Although rare, a raccoon will occasionally climb a tree when held by a grapple, so be sure to look up if you can't find him close by.

A huge added benefit to using grapples and drags is that the trapped critter won't destroy your set. This can save lots of time and energy for the trapper. Additionally, animals that are tangled in brush will be hidden from trap thieves and other nosy folks.

Railroad plates make great drags for raccoon trapping. I rig mine with six feet of chain and a mid-line swivel. Even extra large raccoons find it difficult to get far while dragging a 20-pound iron weight along. If the set location happens to be exceptional, I'll leave the railroad plate behind and use it year after year.

Raccoons in northern climates tend to den up once winter sets in, only to become active again when the temperature climbs. But I've caught raccoons when the mercury was in the single digits, so long as it hadn't been cold for an extended time. Even in prolonged cold weather, raccoons may travel short distances from their dens. I've often caught them in sets adjacent to established trails leading into cornfields during extremely cold conditions.

Bait sets tend to lose much of their attraction during late winter because male raccoons are more interested in finding a mate. You should rely more on a good gland lure at this time and stake your traps solid. By holding a raccoon at your set, especially if it's a female, the sent left behind will help attract other raccoons to the set.

If you've been neglecting raccoons on your trapline you should think again. They are abundant in most areas and relatively easy to take. A decent catch will only add to your profits at the end of the season.

The Crossing Log Set Revisited

I'LL NEVER FORGET the day, back in 1962, that I caught my first fox. I was 14 years old and had been trying to catch a fox for two years with nothing to show for my efforts except a few sprung traps. But as I rounded a bend in the stream that snowy December morning, I could hardly believe my eyes when I spotted a large gray caught by its front paw in my crossing log set.

The idea for the set came from a book called *The Trappers Guide* by O. L. Butcher. And since then, I've continued to use this method to catch gray foxes, raccoons, and other critters over the years. Admittedly, it's not a set designed for the high-speed longliner covering hundreds of miles by vehicle. But it still has its place on some traplines. And once made, the set can be used year after year in all types of weather conditions.

Foxes, especially grays, often use trees that have fallen across streams as a natural bridge to get from one point to another. Once you've located a suitable crossing log, chop out a trap bed with your hand axe deep enough so that your trap, preferably a 1½ coil spring, will lie even with the top of the log after covering it with an inch of fine, rotted wood. There should be plenty of suitable material to cover your trap near the base of the fallen tree. If not, peat moss or cover hulls will work well.

Grab a few twigs the size of pencil stubs and place them under the trap jaws to help stabilize it. Next, when you cover the trap, keep the area between the jaws considerably lower than the surroundings, that way your chances of a fox stepping directly on the pan will increase. A cigar-sized stepping stick in front of the trap will help insure that the fox puts his foot where you want it. Then nail the trap chain to the side of the log and you're done. No bait or lure is necessary.

Although the set might be time consuming to make, once the trap bed has been carved out you'll have a great location that will continue to take foxes for many years. It's a fun, old-time blind set that should fool any fox that happens along, and will also take raccoons, fishers, and many other furbearers.

But if you aren't into nostalgia and hacking trap beds out of solid oak, fear not. Crossing logs are still great locations to set traps for gray foxes, and you should never ignore them. Rather than chop out a bed in the log, you can always make blind sets by digging a trap bed in the dirt at each end of the log where you believe the fox will enter and exit his bridge over troubled water. Don't be afraid to narrow the ends of the log with brush or sticks to force the gray into your traps. They won't mind it a bit. Cover your trap with dry dirt or peat moss and blend it lightly into the surrounding ground cover. I've caught doubles on grays—one at each end—with this setup.

If you prefer using bait and or lure rather than blind sets, you'll still want to look for a few crossing logs on your trapline. A dirthole set located a few feet away from each end of the log will pay big dividends. Location is of primary importance when trapping any species, and since many valuable furbearers use crossing logs, traps set in their vicinity are sure to increase your season's catch.

I often use peat moss to cover my traps, especially when weather conditions promise rain mixed with subfreezing temperatures. The nice thing about peat moss is that it absorbs a tremendous amount of water. When you get one of those days (or weeks) where it rains all afternoon and the temperature plummets at night, you'll find that only the top crust over your trap will be frozen. Simply take your trowel and lift the frozen pancake of peat off your set. The trap will still be in perfect working order. Take a handful of fresh, dry peat moss, sprinkle it liberally over your set, and you're on your way. On windy days, you might want to sift a thin layer of dry dirt over the peat or mix it with cover hulls to keep it from blowing off your trap.

Gray foxes are not difficult to lure into a trap once you figure out where they are traveling. Crossing logs are a sure bet on any trapline, and the sets I've described will add pelts to your stretching boards for many seasons to come.

The Berried Bait Set

THE FARM MANAGER had told me he saw several fox families earlier in summer, and I wondered why they had disappeared. The area I was trapping consisted mostly of grassy fields surrounded by woodlands crisscrossed by several jeep trails. My job was to thin out the red foxes. Trouble was, I couldn't seem to find much sign.

One thing I did see was a lot of coyote droppings along the jeep trails. I'd often read about the devastating effect coyotes can have on a healthy red fox population and concluded that although mange or distemper could have caused their numbers to drop, coyotes were more likely to blame for the sudden decrease in reds.

I decided to run a combination fox and coyote line with traps strong enough for the eastern coyote but at the same time not excessive for fox. The Victor number two coil spring with offset round jaws seemed to fit the bill. Mine were equipped with six inches of heavy, straight link chain attached to the trap's bottom with a double swivel. I file down the pan-notch and square off the dog on my canine traps so they fire on first touch. I also take heavy pliers and turn up the jaw ends where they jut through the bottom of the trap so the big coyotes can't pop them out.

I made six sets at different locations along the jeep trails, but an intersection where two trails crossed a vast open field looked particularly good. Both fox and coyote droppings could be found nearby, so I put in a dirt hole set and a flat set on opposite sides of the intersection. The winds were right, so my lure was sure to work its way toward any fox or coyote traveling either trail.

The next morning I expected a coyote or two but my traps were empty. A light snow had fallen and I could see where a coyote had started to approach the sets but turned back, showing little interest. I had been using meat bait along with a mild gland lure, and it just wasn't enough to stimulate the yodel dog's interest. Figuring a day or two would change my results, I decided to leave things as they were and keep checking the traps until I connected.

Two weeks and one gray fox later, I realized it was time to change my strategy. It wasn't that the coyotes feared my sets or were digging up my traps. They just didn't seem to be interested in the bait or lure I was using. So I decided to use a different attractant.

Again, as before, I put in a dirt hole set and a flat at the intersecting jeep trails that had looked so promising earlier. Making sure that the prevailing winds would carry the scent of my bait toward the trails, I cut a stout branch from a dead tree, hammered it into the ground eight feet from my sets, and smeared a good-sized gob of O'Gorman's Long Distance Call Lure on top of the post at five-feet and another gob two-feet off the ground. Placing the lure high allowed the prevailing winds to carry it farther from my sets. O'Gorman is from Montana, and I wanted a lure made out west hoping the foreign musk would help pique the curiosity of my Pennsylvania coyotes.

I decided to use Nick Wyshinski's Loganberry for bait at both sets. I had never tried it on canines before, but the coyote droppings I'd seen earlier contained plenty of berry seeds, and I wanted to experiment.

The next morning I was happy to see two inches of fresh snow. The white powder would only increase my chances of catching the coyotes that had been avoiding my sets. And as I drove toward the traps, I saw two big males caught by a front foot at each set.

I could see tracks in the snow revealing that several coyotes had broke from the woods and traveled across the field more than 100 yards straight toward my traps. The call lure atop the post had done its job, as the canines had circled the post several times before noticing my sets and moving in. The powerful scent of the berry bait enticed both coyotes into my traps after the long distance lure drew them from afar.

In winter, the odor of fresh berries can be appealing to coyotes and foxes. It's something they haven't had in their diets for a while, and the sweet smell can be irresistible. But fruit baits lose their potency in cold weather and that is why a quality long distance call lure comes in to play.

I often use a nearby tree, fence post, or whatever else might be handy when I place my call lure. The idea is to get it up off the ground where the prevailing winds can distribute the scent over a broad and extended range, thereby significantly increasing your chances of drawing fur into your traps.

Railroad'n the Fox

MUSKRAT SEASON WAS still young, and the sight of my favorite 'rat stream hastened my pace. The sky was crystal clear and a gentle, almost warm, November breeze carried away all perceptions of the troubled outside world.

But as I waded knee deep in the frigid water toward an old familiar cove that had produced countless muskrats over the years, I saw that the area was covered with traps! Human footprints were everywhere: mashed into the stream banks and gouged through feeding stations.

My hopes for a rewarding trapline were suddenly lost. Again, like on so many previous occasions, the high number of competitive trappers in my area had foiled my plans. I shouldn't have been so surprised, as the area had an inexhaustible supply of novice muskrat trappers. I'd either have to try another type of trapping or settle for seconds on the muskrat line.

The year was 1966, and my brother John and I made plans to trap foxes for the remainder of the winter. The fox was seldom molested in our area so we felt confident of finding suitable numbers to warrant trapping them.

The following morning found us heading to a location we used for cleaning our traps. There was a tiny spring hidden in a wooded valley that would provide us with water for boiling. The easiest way to reach it was by walking the railroad tracks that sliced through the adjacent meadows.

After pulling our trap-cooking supplies from the trunk, which consisted of two iron support bars, a sturdy metal pot, a pound of logwood crystals and a dozen traps, we started walking along the railroad tracks toward the stream.

Along the way, John noticed some red fox droppings between two ties. We examined them and discovered that the fox had been dining primarily on rabbits. We didn't travel much farther before finding many additional droppings scattered about. John and I soon realized that the foxes were using the railroad as a regular portion of their daily route, just as they would follow a farm lane or some other type of trail. It appeared we were in some fine fox country, so we decided to begin our trapline in the surrounding fields.

After reaching the spring, I prepared the traps, inspecting each one to be certain it would function properly, while John prospected for set locations. My boil pot, filled with spring water, was perched upon the two iron bars, which were stretched across rocks that circled the fire I built. As the water began to boil, I slipped twigs between the trap jaws before dropping them into the water so the insides would be coated with dye, too.

John had been gone only one hour but had found several excellent set locations, and the longer he spoke of his findings, the more excited we became.

When the traps were done cooking, we lifted them from the scalding pot and hung them in nearby saplings to dry. It was still early morning by the time we made our way from the tiny stream back toward the railroad.

We soon came to a short-cropped field that dropped off at both sides of the railroad. The tracks would provide a perfect observation point for any hunting fox, so I walked down into the field and set my packbasket beside me. My rubber gloves were neatly arranged on top of the other gear for easy access. I slipped them on and rubbed a few drops of fox urine into them. To successfully trap foxes, one must keep the set smelling foxy, so the fox will be less cautious upon investigating in his usual, timid fashion. Any additional lures or baits must be isolated from contact with your gloves, traps, or other equipment. The purpose of a lure or bait is to draw the fox over your trap while he forages for it. If these odors emerge on your trap, the fox may consequently dig directly into it, resulting in a sprung trap.

I grasped my 16-inch digging trowel and bored a small hole in the ground about four inches wide by ten inches deep. I dug the hole in a 45-degree angle so the fox would have to approach from the front to see into it. Then I carved a bed for my trap directly in front of the hole.

The trap, a 1-½ double coil spring, had been stained with black logwood dye to mask the odor of steel and help prevent it from rusting.

The odor of steel or rust around a set will tip off any fox that has been caught in a trap before. Otherwise, they don't fear these odors. I've followed their tracks into neighboring dumps teeming with scraps of iron and rusty tin cans and have seen where they crawl through tiny openings in wire fences without hesitation. And when the snow piles high along the railroad tracks, they tiptoe on the iron rails rather than trudge through the heavy white powder. Having said that, the odor of steel at a hole supposedly dug by another fox is not a good idea, as a fox might dig up your trap out of sheer curiosity.

After driving an iron stake underground to anchor my trap, I pressed the trap firmly into loose soil in the bed so it wouldn't wobble if the fox stepped on a spring or jaw, then I scooped all the loose dirt into my sifting screen and shook it over the bare trap so only the fine dirt would filter over the trap to conceal it. I never use any kind of cover when I bury a trap. Instead, I file the pan notch and the tip of the trigger for faster action. If it sets low enough, there is little chance any dirt will clog under the pan to prevent it from firing.

After my set is completely covered, I scrape a low spot over the center of the trap, a kind of swale, so to speak. This causes the fox to step between the jaws, which are buried under heavier dirt.

Finally, I was ready for the finishing touch. An egg-size piece of tainted woodchuck was placed in the hole, and my favorite gland lure, used sparingly, trickled down inside. A few well-aimed squirts of fox urine from my plastic squeeze bottle soaked the dirt covering my trap.

Trap set with dog facing hole is best

Trap covered with swale so fox must step down

I stood up, grabbed my packbasket, and slung it over one shoulder. Then I brushed up the grass I'd been kneeling on and walked directly away. From start to finish, the entire operation took less than ten minutes. I like to leave the set rough looking, just as a fox would.

John made our next dirt hole set by a narrow wooded island in the center of a grassy field. We knew the foxes would hunt the area, as it was a good hideout for mice, rabbits, and other game.

A saddle in a broad meadow bordering a tract of woods yielded our next set location. Foxes, like people, are always looking for the easier travel routes and will cut through a basin between two knolls rather than go over them to get from point A to B. I completed another dirt hole set in the center of this low area and we continued on.

Within a couple hours we had six sets out and felt they were sufficient for the area. Each trap had been placed in key locations that we felt would produce foxes.

The following morning, it was pitch black as we approached the ridge that held our first trap. And when John trained his flashlight on the set, there was no guessing—the trap was empty.

When we neared the small patch of woods bordering our second set, we saw our first red fox of the season. Our set would be improved by the captured fox as the odors he left behind would help draw other foxes into it.

The last four sets were empty but we were satisfied with just one fox for the day.

The following morning, as we began our hike up the ridge to our first set, I heard the faint sound of clinking steel.

John hadn't heard anything, but when I told him I thought we had a fox, our pace quickened. Within seconds we were face to face with a beautiful red. I stood back and held the flashlight while John removed the fox and re-created the set.

It was still dark as we approached the patch of woods that had produced our first fox of the season, and when we reached the set, we found another red fox waiting for us. The morning progressed rapidly, and we finished the line with just enough time to reach our vehicles and get to school. We had two nice reds and very high hopes for the following day's trapline.

On the third morning we took another fox. Our set on the ridge had nailed a female red. At first, we thought the fox was sick, as it lay motionless in our trap. I cautiously approached with the flashlight shining directly on the fox and soon realized she'd been shot neatly in the head by a small caliber firearm. Apparently someone had been hunting nearby and noticed the fox in our trap.

It's not uncommon to have foxes stolen from traps or find the animal's body riddled with shotgun pellets. But this person, whom we had never met, humanely killed our fox as an act of good sportsmanship.

Five more days drifted slowly by and our traps along the railroad remained empty. There hadn't been any snow, so we were unable to determine if foxes were visiting them. To be safe, we decided to pull the line and head for new territory. But as we journeyed down the railroad for the last time, a red fox suddenly burst up in front of us at our first set, firmly secured in our trap. The fox was fully prime, displaying deep rich colors of red and black with a snow-white underbelly.

A fox had visited our second set by the patch of woods that night but never got close enough to step in our trap. His tracks were abundant in the loose soil surrounding it. Apparently, he had caught the scent of the other foxes that were caught. He was still free, and that assured us that future generations of foxes would be in the area.

The rest of our sets remained empty until we reached the last one, which held a large red fox by two toes. He was pumping the trap hard, and I didn't think he'd stay caught much longer. We hurried toward him but the weight of our winter coats and heavy boots hampered our pace. Meanwhile, the fox hadn't slowed down at all. He continued to jerk and pull at the trap in a frantic attempt to escape.

I reached the trap just as the fox broke free and came tumbling into my legs. Luckily, he didn't bite me before bolting toward the woods. Thinking I might catch him, I began running too, but the fox soon hurtled a small brook and melted into the shadowed forest.

I dropped to the ground exhausted and laid on my back. Daybreak had come, and with it a bleak, gray sky. The fox was gone; all was quiet save the muffled pounding of John's footsteps as he ran toward me. Soon I could hear the squeaking of his boots and his heavy breathing.

"Are you all right Bill?" he breathed. "Did the fox bite you?"

"I'm fine." I said. "But you must think I'm crazy for chasing that fox the way I did."

John chuckled. "Actually, I thought you might catch him for a minute there."

"Me too," I said. "That ol' fox sure got an education!"

John looked in the direction the fox had run and nodded. "He sure did. And I don't care that he got away so much; I just hope he doesn't give his pups any trapping instructions."

The Mulch Set

Much has been written over the years about trap shy foxes, and I've encountered my share of them in the last five decades. But I'll never forget one particular fox whose antics both surprised and baffled me for weeks until I finally outsmarted the critter.

It all started when a landowner called to complain that a fox was killing his free roaming chickens. It had taken over a dozen in just two days, burying their feathered carcasses all over his property.

When I arrived at the farm, I managed to locate several good set locations within a short time. The landowner was concerned about his remaining fowl, so I advised him to keep the birds confined for a day or two, certain that I'd have the culprit in my traps by then. It was autumn, and trapping conditions were ideal. A game trail leading into the woods from the farm seemed like the perfect place to snag the fox. Its droppings marked the trail in several places, so I decided to punch in two quick dirt hole sets, one on each side of it.

I set my packbasket beside me, slipped on a pair of rubber gloves, and pulled out a 1½ double coil spring. The trap's pan-notch and dog were filed for a crisp release, and only six inches of chain was attached to the trap's base with a double swivel. This rig will prevent the fox from making powerful lunges that could aid in its escape and it keeps foot damage to a minimum

With the hole dug and the trap firmly bedded, I covered it with loose soil and scraped a depression over the pan. An egg-size piece of beaver meat was placed in the hole along with a few drops of gland lure.

The second set was a carbon copy of the first. I had used this simple method many times before and was confident I'd have a fox or two the following day.

But the next morning I returned only to find my traps partially uncovered and, adding insult to injury, a smoking fresh fox dropping accompanied each trap. It was obvious that the fox wasn't impressed with my sets.

A urine post set might work, I thought. With a well-blended trap, this set can fool even the most experienced canine. I sprinkled some fresh dirt over my exposed traps, hoping they might still connect, and followed the trail farther into the woods until I came to a small tree stump that begged for a trap at its base. I dug a trap bed next to the stump and drove a rebar stake dead center into the bed with my trap attached. Next, I nestled in a double coil spring and made sure to bed it tight so it wouldn't wobble if the fox stepped on a jaw. I covered it with a thin layer of dirt so it was level with the ground and sprinkled dead leaves over the dirt to blend with the surroundings. After pouring an ounce of fox urine onto the tree stump I walked away.

The next day I had a large male red fox waiting for me. The landowner was thrilled and immediately decided to leave his chickens, ducks, and other fowl out of their pens, although I warned him that it was mating season and that another fox may be lurking about, but he went ahead and released them anyway.

The next morning several chickens had been killed along with his prize 25-pound turkey. To make matters worse, my traps were empty with both dirthole sets dug up again. I suspected that I'd be dealing with a very spooky fox from here on.

For two weeks, I tried every trick I knew to catch the fox. Nothing would work. It would either ignore my sets or, depending on its mood, I suppose, proceed to dig them up. It seemed impossible to fool the fox, and I was beginning to think I'd never catch it. But when the landowner called me about a deer killed by a car near his property, I hung up the phone and went directly to his farm.

There was an area on the property the size of a small bedroom where a mass of oak leaves had blown into a fence corner. I dragged the deer carcass into the leaves (check state game laws before possessing highway killed wildlife) and buried it under a foot of the brown mulch. Next, I raked out two narrow paths leading to the carcass with my feet. I bedded a trap solidly in each path and covered them with a thin layer of leaves. It was impossible to see where the traps were hidden. A stepping stick was placed ahead of each trap, and I was careful not to use any lure or scent.

The following morning I had a female red staring up at me from the pile of mulch. Obviously the mate of the big male I'd captured weeks before. The landowner never had a problem with foxes after that day and was eternally grateful, granting me trapping rights for life on his property.

The Mulch Set won't always be feasible on every trapline, and conditions must be right in order to use it, but variations of the set are as limitless as your imagination, and it should fool even the most wary canine on your trapline.

Trapping the Suburbs

I GREW UP in southeastern Pennsylvania, twenty miles from the Philadelphia county line. There was a lot more open land back then, although a huge suburban sprawl had begun to overtake the area and things were changing rapidly. I watched the farms and woodlands of my youth become devoured at a frightening pace as wealthy developers gobbled up every acre they could get their hands on. New houses, industrial parks, and business complexes soon dotted the landscape wherever I turned.

And with the new homes came new people: city folks, many of whom were deeply opposed to trapping because they perceived it as an act of barbarism. It became more difficult to trap the outskirts of these newly developed areas with each passing year. Suburbanites routinely tampered with my traps, thinking they were doing good by saving a critter from some nasty old trapper; and free roaming pets seemed everywhere, which meant more incidental catches then I could tolerate. What's more, Pennsylvania law prohibits trapping within 150 yards of occupied buildings, which made finding places for legal sets more challenging with each passing year.

But having said that, there were still plenty of furbearers in spite of all the new buildings. My primary targets were muskrats, raccoons, and foxes; and their numbers were on the rise. Most streams were teeming with muskrats, and raccoon populations bordered on infestation in certain areas; in fact, many were living in the attics and chimneys of unsuspecting townsfolk. And foxes, especially reds, could be found in large numbers throughout the remaining open fields.

I wanted to continue catching fur, but the bulk of my trapping grounds had been obliterated by hulking bulldozers that seemed to lurk everywhere. Although the big machines had taken their toll, there was still considerable real estate that hadn't been touched. Golf courses, country clubs, state parks, and large private estates soon became my new trapping territory. And I caught a lot of fur in these areas over several decades.

As suburban sprawl slowly pushes birds and animals out of their home range, the remaining fields and woodlots become saturated with relocated wildlife, producing high numbers of furbearers per square acre.

Almost any small stream becomes a natural corridor, too, and when these streams pass through road culverts in metropolitan areas they become deadly locations that produce fur all season long.

Abandoned buildings are another good fur producer. Sometimes farms are sold to developers only to sit for years before anything happens. Vacant barns tend to draw raccoons like magnets. Their floors are often littered with droppings as these masked marauders move in and take up residence. Don't pass them up; sometimes a single building will produce a dozen or more prime pelts.

Golf courses can be an additional bonanza for the metropolitan trapper. They are outstanding locations for muskrats due to the soft banks and lush vegetation surrounding the streams and ponds. Thousands of dollars are spent each year to keep the grounds in shape, and the last thing a greenskeeper wants to see is muskrats tearing into the banks and digging up valuable turf. Most golf courses welcome trappers with open arms, and some excellent trapping can be had simply by asking permission. Once you get a foot in the door, ask for consent to trap foxes and raccoons too. You might be surprised at how many you'll catch as an added bonus to your muskrat line.

There are advantages to trapping private estates, too, not the least of which is a lack of competition. And because most estates are posted or fenced off, you needn't be concerned with bunny-huggers or neighborhood children "finding" your traps, even though you'll be operating within their midst.

When inquiring about permission to trap, introduce yourself by first telling the landowner your name and ask if they are experiencing problems with nuisance wildlife. If so, explain that you would be happy to alleviate the problem and clarify how you intend to do it.

I found that by knocking or a few doors while dressed in clean khakis or jeans and a button-down shirt, I soon had plenty of places to trap. Everybody loves a bargain, even wealthy people. And although they could afford to pay any price to have raccoons removed from their property, they liked the free service I was offering.

Don't be afraid to show the property owner a trap if he seems squeamish about it. Some folks envision the common foothold trap as some barbaric device that crushes an animal's leg with powerful, toothed jaws. Show them a common foothold trap and they will usually change their tune. Bring along a rubber jawed trap too. It could be the key to some valuable trapping territory. Just be sure to have enough of these traps on hand if the landowner wants you to use them.

Don't forget to mention a little about your background. If you trap other estates in the area, say so. This is important because it tells folks that you are established and trusted by their neighbors. If you live in the area, be sure to say so, and always give them your phone number once you've been granted permission to trap.

The first property in a given area is usually the most difficult when seeking permission to trap. There is always the suspicion that you may be a fraud: someone posing as a trapper, who really wants to do them future harm. Hence, I would always start close to my home so I could provide well-known references to prospective property owners. Once I had my first property, I'd mention that person's name to the next landowner on my list. The fact that I was trapping a neighbor's property made it much easier for me to get permission, and I used this method in a kind of domino effect to garner more land than I could effectively trap in a single season.

Once I had approval to trap raccoons I immediately asked about muskrats and foxes. I was never turned down. These large estates soon became trapline paradises for me. Each one a solitude from the hustle and bustle of the outside world, as I had no worries about competitive trappers or people tampering with my sets.

I asked people to keep their dogs and cats inside or on a leash while trapping on their property. I also asked if any neighbors had free-roaming pets, because the last thing I needed while trapping in suburbia (or anywhere else for that matter) was to catch someone's cat or dog.

We can't always keep wandering pets from our traps, but there are things we can do to lessen the possibility: I'll often use fruit baits when trapping raccoons and foxes in metropolitan areas because these baits are not attractive to cats. Also, traps set in water, even when baited with fish, will keep all but the hungriest housecat away. Urine post sets will keep most dogs, with their longer legs, from blundering into them, and dirt hole sets used in conjunction with fruit baits usually won't attract dogs but often work well on fox, and even coyotes, in late fall and winter.

Another obstacle for the suburban trapper to contend with is domestic waterfowl. Often, permission to trap is granted only if you can assure the landowner you won't harm the waterfowl that they've grown so attached to.

This is risky at best, so I never make an absolute promise that I won't catch a duck or goose. If that means I don't get permission to trap, so be it. What I do in this case is assure the owner that it's unlikely that I'll catch any waterfowl based on my experience and the type of sets I intend to use. If they want their nuisance wildlife problem resolved, and most of them do, they'll usually agree to let me trap.

In these situations, I only set my muskrat traps at underwater dens and slide my foothold traps up inside the entrance. Sometimes I'll use bodygrippers if the den is deep enough to preclude the likelihood of a duck or goose sticking its head into my traps. Although I've never caught any domestic waterfowl using these methods, there is no guarantee it won't happen some day.

Mink can be taken in pocket sets provided your trap is set far enough inside the pocket so that a duck or goose won't stick its head into the trap while searching for something to eat. Raccoon traps set in water must be deep. By targeting their hind feet, with traps set in at least eight inches of water, you should be okay. But since raccoons can readily be taken on land, I keep my sets away from water when I'm concerned about catching ducks and geese.

Metropolitan areas provide many good locations for traps. One doesn't have to limit a trapline to golf courses and estate properties. Just keep in mind that there are so many people around, your chances of having traps stolen or sprung by neighborhood do-gooders is greatly increased.

A good way to help prevent this is to keep traps away from areas where people may be hiking. Dogs often accompany hikers, and they may be attracted to your set. Also, keep in mind that many states require that traps and snares be set a certain distance from buildings.

A good rule of the road for suburban trappers is to use drags, grapples, or drowning sets when feasible so your catch is less likely to be discovered by anyone.

I dye my traps brown rather than black to conceal them from nosy people. Brown seems to blend better in the muddy waters of suburbia. I break up the outline of the trap by pushing silt around the jaws or by draping a soggy leaf or some other light vegetation over the trap. I also conceal my bodygrippers by dressing their jaws with long strands of grass. Simple added touches such as these, greatly reduce trap visibility, which is crucial in metropolitan areas.

Although the metro trapper may be forced to pass up some outstanding fur pockets because they are surrounded by too many homes, all is not lost. Residential areas are often connected to vacant fields, neighboring estates, and intersecting waterways where your traps can draw in a considerable number of these furbearers.

In many suburban areas the raccoon has become public enemy number one, and it's not uncommon to see one infected with rabies or distemper staggering close to homes in broad daylight. When this happens, folks assume every raccoon they see is sick and become very fearful of them. Because the surrounding woodlands have been cut down to make room for more houses, and den trees all but eliminated, raccoons adopt human habitat as their own, and begin denning in chimneys and sewers. Soon their nighttime raids on garbage cans become intolerable, and people just want them out.

Large suburban estates like the ones I trapped were often overrun with raccoons because their ivy-covered homes with their expansive roofs and multiple chimneys were attractive to pregnant females.

Most of my raccoons were caught in combination fox/coon sets since both frequented the same fields and woods. My dirthole sets were dug a bit deep to keep raccoons from reaching into the hole, and I placed them along the edges of wooded areas bordering fields and openings in brush rows and fences.

I always made multiple sets at openings in hedgerows where one estate property bordered another, especially if prevailing winds would carry the scent of my call lure toward the neighboring land. This helped me draw in foxes and raccoons from adjoining estates without doing a lot of extra legwork. Essentially, I was trapping the bulk of two properties simply by setting close to their boundary lines. It wasn't uncommon for me to catch doubles or triples using this method, and I was able to clean up several large estates in short order.

One particular morning I approached a location where I'd made three dirthole sets only to discover my first trap surrounded by six horses. One held its head so low it almost touched the ground, and my heart began to pound as I thought it might have its tongue caught in my trap. But as I walked closer, the horses slowly began to back away, and I saw they'd been investigating a red fox caught in my trap. It was sprawled out flat on its side, motionless, and I wondered if it had been trampled to death. In the woods behind the fox were two more sets. Each held raccoons, alive and well.

I walked directly to the fox. There was no blood anywhere and the pelt looked good. Perhaps it was still salvageable. I bent over, grabbed a hind leg, and started to turn the fox over when it suddenly came alive! Baring a mouthful of pointy teeth, the feisty red narrowly missed taking a chunk out of my hand. I jumped back in the nick of time, thankful that my trap was rigged with only a six-inch chain. It had been sound asleep the whole time! The fox was never harmed by the curious horses.

After dispatching the fox and both raccoons, I moved to an abandoned barn in the adjoining field where I had made five sets the day before. The barn, like most abandoned buildings in the area, was loaded with raccoon droppings. The floors were literally covered with scat, and it was obvious they'd inhabited the place for years.

Five Dirthole sets produced three prime bandits, and I was very happy with the day thus far. I had staked my traps solid rather than using grapples because I didn't want to risk losing a raccoon somewhere inside the barn. After remaking my sets, I moved on to a narrow stream where I had two pocket sets.

I had dug the pockets high into the bank so the raccoon would have to stand on its hind feet to investigate. I wanted a hind foot catch, even though I was using a drag, because raccoons will sometimes chew on a front foot after it grows numb in the trap's jaws. One of my traps was missing, but as I scanned the surrounding brush for a tangled coon I found nothing. They're usually close by, but that was not the case here. I searched and searched, and was about to give up, when I saw movement from the corner of my eye. Looking up, I discovered my raccoon had climbed a small tree and tangled in my trap. That was the first and last time I ever had that happen, and I'm glad for it, as I spent more time than I care to admit getting the critter down.

I ended the day with six raccoons, two red fox, and a half dozen muskrats. The landowner was elated when I stopped to show him my catch. By season's end, I had taken a dozen reds, 20 raccoons, and 15 muskrats from his five-acre property.

I no longer live near a suburban area, but when I did, my season average ran from 90 to 100 raccoons, several dozen fox and bushels of muskrats while holding down a full time job.

High numbers of furbearers are often found within urban areas across the country. In fact, acre for acre, more critters roam through suburbia than in many wilderness and farm regions. Consequently, the suburban trapper can make some decent cash by knocking on a few doors in these areas.

So if you live near a metropolitan area and never considered trapping there because you thought it had nothing to offer, think again! There's money to be made in that asphalt jungle.

Animal Damage Control

As an animal damage control trapper, you can continue to earn money from trapping long after the regular fur season ends. Suburban dwellers are willing to pay big bucks to have wildlife pests removed from their property. So much so that a $15 raccoon can easily quadruple in value when it's removed from someone's house for a fee.

Of course, your potential for earnings from animal damage control (ADC) depends largely upon how close you are to metropolitan areas, especially the suburban outskirts where the majority of upper middle-class folks live these days. In rural areas, people are more apt to handle their own problems because they're more familiar with wild critters and know how to deal with them.

Before starting an ADC sideline or full-time business, be sure to check your state wildlife laws. Most states require that you obtain a permit or license first. You may even have to pass an exam or obtain special training at your own expense prior to receiving your license. Other states simply require that you submit a fee, renewable annually, and that you adhere to their regulations governing wildlife control.

I've met a number of ADC trappers over the years that keep their businesses booming without spending a fortune on advertising. They get the word out by visiting police departments, animal shelters, zoo officials, township supervisors, and conservation officers in their area, asking them to refer complaints their way. Many of these agencies are happy to accommodate them.

Although there are many new devices on today's market for capturing suburban pests while excluding dogs and cats, I still recommend the time-proven wooden box trap. Cage traps are good too, but they let the world know what's in them, and when animals are visible they become an attraction to some people, especially curious child who might stick a finger into a cage trap and be bitten. Animals often injure themselves while fighting cage traps, which is another reason why I don't like them. Snares, foothold traps, and other devices present similar problems, although they all have their place in animal damage control.

Solid box traps keep nosey neighbors and curious children away because they can't see what's inside. Captured animals feel more secure when enclosed in a solid box trap and usually won't injure themselves trying to fight their way out. And solid traps are particularly valuable when trapping nuisance skunks, as they are less inclined to spray if they can't see a target.

Rubber-jawed traps are designed to reduce stress to a captured animal's foot and are an asset to many kinds of suburban animal control work. Keep in mind that these traps still exert enough pressure to restrict blood circulation. During extremely cold weather, an animal's foot could freeze below the jaws. It could be someone's pet.

Bodygripping traps work well when you can be certain of your target. The springs should be in perfect working order to ensure a quick kill, and in some instances may have to be beefed up to accomplish this. One major advantage of killer traps is that they eliminate any chance of escape or additional property damage once the animal is caught. The major drawback, of course, is that they can't be used if there is any chance of catching someone's pet.

Snares are great tools for suburban animal damage control. They are inexpensive and work almost anywhere. When fixed with relaxing locks they offer less chance of injury to domestic animals that could blunder into your set. In suburbia, snares work especially well at den entrances and openings in fences and other manmade structures.

I use 3/32" by 7x7 galvanized aircraft cable for all my snares. It offers a nice loop and has tremendous holding power. I'll often take a length of soft, nine gauge wire, bend a three-inch-long V into one end and push it into the ground to form a quick support for hanging my snare.

The opposite end of the support wire (above photo) is bent into an inverted W, which acts as a clasp to hold my snare in place. I weave my snare cable through the W and then set my loop dead center of the animal's travel way with the support wire several inches to the side. I leave my snare lock run slightly down hill to promote quick close-ups for a neck catch.

Be sure to stake your snare away from den entrances or openings into solid structures so a captured animal cannot crawl inside and wedge itself solid, making it difficult to retrieve.

Once you've captured a target animal, you must remove it from the location, dead or alive. Some states require ADC trappers to kill certain known rabies carriers like skunks and raccoons. Barring this, your customer may request that you relocate their nuisance critter alive. Be prepared and have the necessary resources to accommodate both circumstances. Relocating live wildlife generally requires transporting the critter a considerable distance away as well as an additional trap to replace the one with your catch still inside. Finding a place to release nuisance animals where they won't return or bother someone else can be time consuming. Time is money and you might want to consider charging extra for this service.

When I want to relocate an animal, a catch pole helps me control the critter while removing it from traps or snares. I also use it to help place animals into cages or burlap bags for live transport. Burlap bags work well because they are inexpensive and easy to store. Most animals relax once inside, and the few feisty ones that want to fight, can't seem to claw or chew through them. They work especially well for transporting live beavers too. Just be sure the animal gets plenty of airflow once in your vehicle.

Sometimes a catch pole is all you'll need to answer a complaint, especially if it concerns a sick or injured animal that happens to be lying in someone's doorway. I relied on a Ketch-All Pole for over 30 years. They are a bit more expensive than other animal release poles but are worth their weight in gold to the serious animal control trapper. These sturdy poles can extend themselves for a long reach and are extremely durable.

But catch poles, no matter what brand, are useless when dealing with skunks. This is where a syringe pole makes all the difference in the world. You can make one yourself or purchase it commercially. For a long while, I used a four-foot-long wooden dowel (broom handles also work) and two L-shaped clamps that I made from thin pieces of sheet metal. The long portions of each "L" were screwed into the end of the dowel with the short ends overlapping the tip with just enough space to wedge the syringe's plunger between the metal and the wooden tip. It worked for years, but eventually I purchased a commercial syringe pole through one of the many ADC suppliers that advertise on the Internet. It was worth every penny.

There are numerous skunk dispatch kits on the market as well, including chemicals for lethal injection; however, I like to use a veterinary grade muscle-relaxing drug. This way I only inject 1/2 cc into the skunk's neck and the animal becomes immobilized within seconds. Check with your state's laws regarding these drugs, as licensing for their use is required.

I've injected dozens of live skunks with a syringe pole without being sprayed. The trick is to use a thin needle (I use 20-gauge) and approach the skunk on foot, very slowly. Once I'm within four feet, I inch my syringe toward the skunk's face. I want it to see what's coming. I pause when the needle is close so the skunk can sniff at it awhile. Once the skunk satisfies its curiosity, I ease the needle into its neck or rump. Because I'm directly behind the pole and can't see the plunger move, I watch the skunk as I push in the needle. I know the drug is injected once the critter is pushed slightly backward by the gentle force of my pole, which signals that my plunger has bottomed out.

I've removed skunks from buildings, traps, snares, cages, window wells, and just about every conceivable other place with this method. As long as you move slowly, and stop cold if the skunk acts nervous or raises its tail, you will find the same success I have.

Another common suburban pest is the raccoon. Generally, they will either be pregnant or have already had their young when you get the complaint. Raccoons get into chimneys by climbing up to the roof via downspouts, the corners of buildings, or overhanging branches. Then they straddle the inside of the chimney by pushing out with all four legs while descending to the damper where the young are eventually born.

Many trappers are charging an additional fee to install chimney caps after removing raccoons, thereby receiving double what they would ordinarily make on the complaint. Additionally, some are offering to clean out the chimney for even greater profits.

Raccoons in attics present another opportunity to earn extra money. After removing the raccoon (again, checking for cubs) the attic will usually be in need of repair due to raccoon droppings, dislodged and torn insulation, or holes torn through the roof. Many homeowners, if pleased with your services, may be inclined to hire you for the additional work.

Although skunks and raccoons will make up the bulk of nuisance wildlife complaints in most suburban areas, groundhogs, squirrels, muskrats, and beavers will also be high on the list.

Groundhogs are easily removed with the snaring system I mentioned previously. If you can't find a den entrance or fence opening for a snare, your best bet is to use a box trap baited with fresh, leafy vegetables.

Squirrels are a common nuisance in suburban areas. They often invade homes when cold weather sets in, gnawing through walls or overhangs to gain entrance. An effective method for trapping squirrels inside buildings is to use a common rattrap baited with peanut butter. Simply nail the trap vertically to a wooden post or some other suitable structure in the building, bait side down. If you set the trap on the attic floor, be sure to have it backed into a corner with the baited end facing forward so the squirrel can't approach from the rear and be thrown clear by the kill bar when its triggered.

Muskrats play an important role in the annual income of many suburban ADC trappers. Most damage complaints occur in fall and spring when trapping season is open. Trappers usually welcome the opportunity to cash in on their pelts as a bonus to the fee they charge for removing these rodents from properties.

Many suburban areas also have problems with beavers plugging culverts and gnawing down expensive ornamental trees. There are cage traps on the market for these giant rodents but they are very expensive

I use snares for all suburban beaver complaints. They are relatively safe (but not foolproof) around youngsters and pets, and keep the beaver alive so I can relocate it if I want to restock an old pond for future fur trapping in winter. I use my Ketch-All pole to hold the beaver down while injecting a muscle-relaxing chemical into its rump with a standard syringe and an 18-gauge needle. Next, I put the groggy flattail into a large burlap bag where it will get enough air to stay comfortable for a few hours until relocated. If I don't want to inject the beaver, I'll have someone hold the burlap bag open for me while I place it inside with my catch pole. Medium sized perforated trashcans can also be used in place of burlap bags. In hot weather, be sure to keep the can or burlap cool.

So, if you hate to see the trapping season end each year, instead of hanging up those traps, put them to good use by catching nuisance wildlife. That way you can trap year round and add to your annual income while you're at it. Life just doesn't get any better than that.

First Time for Beaver

THE ALARM CLOCK shrieked, and I jumped from my warm bed onto the cold floor. Vivid thoughts of furs and trapping flashed through my mind, for it was the first day of the 1971 beaver season. Even with only one hour's sleep, I felt fresh and alive as I pushed open a window and peered into February's crisp, midnight air.

My wife was preparing eggs and bacon, so I hurriedly dressed and entered the kitchen with a cheerful hello. She nodded in my direction, a sleepy smile on her pretty face. While eating, I discussed my plans with her and promised to phone each night. I knew she would worry since this was gong to be a three-day trip.

The short drive to my twin brother John's house was rather unusual as there wasn't any traffic. The small town was sleeping and travel was easy. A light shined brightly through his kitchen window when I pulled up. I tapped on the door, trying not to arouse his family, when his English setter exploded into vicious barks. I heard John's wife shush the dog and start to open the door. Upon discovering it was me, the setter did his usual wild dance until I reassured him with a pat on the head.

John was standing in the kitchen with a cup of coffee in his hand. His eyes strained to stay open. He had been to a farewell party for a fellow employee and hadn't any sleep at all that night.

After throwing his gear into the back of my car, we were soon on our way north to an area we had prospected earlier for beaver sign. A recent snow made the roads slippery, and driving became progressively worse the farther north we traveled. Deer frequently darted across our path, causing me to slow down even more. But five hours later, we had managed to come within 30 miles of our destination. Unfortunately, those final miles proved to be the worst part of our journey as the roads became more and more treacherous.

As the sun began its gradual sweep across the snow-bound mountains and fields, the temperature moderated into the 40-degree range and the white countryside began to sparkle in the morning sun. We had come to a narrow little road that looked more like a bobsled track, for snow was plowed six feet high on both sides. It meandered through miles of prime beaver country. In many areas the road was too narrow for more than one car to squeeze by, but traffic was almost nonexistent, so there was little need for worry. Finally, our nameless, frozen road shot straight toward some rolling mountains, ambled down a small hill and cut through a timbered valley. It was here that the two beaver ponds we intended to trap nestled well hidden from passing motorists. Parking facilities were provided by a snowplow that had turned around in the driveway of a long abandoned farm. My compact car snuggled in perfectly with little room to spare, and John and I hopped out, stiff from our long ride.

We grabbed a half dozen Number 4 Montgomery traps, an ice auger, a hand ax, two shovels, some nails, wire, and other essentials from the trunk and set off.

Our first step off the roadside was more of a plunge, as we sank to our knees in white powder. Having no snowshoes, we expected a rough trip and we got it. Each step became a deliberate effort as we pushed though the snow at a slow, steady pace. Walking didn't get any easier until we reached the first pond. Its frozen surface was barely covered with snow, as strong winds had blown most of it clear. Here we moved easily and soon arrived at a huge beaver lodge.

John slipped off the heavy packbasket with a groan of relief and placed it beside him. In a hurry to get started, I reached inside to grab the ice auger and gouged my thumb into its razor-sharp blade. I felt little pain but could see I was cut deeply by the amount of blood I was losing. Dread washed over me as I visualized an end to our day due to my carelessness. Applying pressure to the wound, I glanced over at John, whose expression showed more concern for my welfare than time lost on the trapline. We both realized my cut was serious and began heading back to the car.

The closest medical facility was at a small hospital in New York, eight miles away. Once we arrived, we had to wait two hours before I was treated. The doctor stitched up my wound, gave me a tetanus shot, and charged me $24 (equal to a week's groceries back then), which stung even more than the auger did.

When we finally returned to the beaver lodge it was late afternoon and we still had to construct our entire set from scratch. Searching for a place to drill our hole, we noticed a few chewed branches extending beyond the ice, which marked the beaver's feeding area. We decided to place our set near the feed bed so when the beaver got hungry and swam toward his submerged food supply, he would see our bait.

I kicked away some snow as John brought over the bloodstained auger. He placed the blade against the heavy ice and pressed down hard on the top of the handle while I grasped the crank firmly with both hands and turned it. With this method, and plenty of muscle, we were able to bore through 24 inches of ice in about 20 minutes. Since the auger had only a six-inch blade, we made four holes for each set and knocked out the center of the ice square with our ax.

Next, we gathered material for our pole set. I found a suitable dead branch to serve as the pole, and after trimming it smooth, started back toward the lodge with it. Along the way, I grabbed a sturdy forked stick for a trap base and cut some fresh poplar branches the thickness of my thumb for bait. I peeled off sections of green bark to reveal the white inner wood so it would catch be beaver's eye as he swam about in his dark, underwater world.

With the exception of the bait, all the wood used for my set was dead. Otherwise, the beaver might decide to gnaw on the pole or another vital part of the set and ruin it.

Back at the beaver lodge, I shoved the long pole through the hole we had drilled until it touched bottom, then I pushed it into the soft mud and spun it around so a mark would appear. When I pulled the pole up I could see exactly where to place my trap platform. The trap and bait would be halfway between the bottom of the ice and the top of the mud below, so the beaver would have a better chance of seeing the bait.

Author with pole set at beaver lodge (1971)

After wiring my Y-shaped stick horizontally to the pole I rested my trap on the forked portion and wired it only enough to keep the trap from wobbling if the beaver bumped it. Once caught, he could easily pull the trap from its base without destroying it. Next I wired my bait just high enough so that it wouldn't clog the trap's jaws as they closed. Then I secured an evergreen bough to the pole behind the bait to keep the beaver from approaching the rear of the set.

I slid the pole back into the water. It was long enough so that two feet stuck above the ice. I wired a cross-log to the pole so a captured beaver couldn't drag it under, then I covered the hole with snow to keep the set from freezing over heavily.

The next lodge was on the opposite side of the pond, about a hundred yards away. As we approached, we saw red fox tracks in the snow. The fox had been hunting mice and stopped to dig under a rotted tree. He then went directly to the beaver lodge and pawed around the sides, hoping to discover a sleeping field mouse. Discouraged finally, he left the pond to hunt the surrounding fields.

John and I now gave all our attention to the new lodge. We picked out a likely spot and drilled through the ice. Unfortunately, once we subtracted the ice thickness from our hole, there wasn't enough water for a pole set. We spent an hour making four separate test holes but the water was too shallow wherever we drilled. By now, darkness was setting in, so we reluctantly decided to call it a day.

When the alarm went off at 5:30 the next morning, John and I almost leaped out of our beds. The excitement of our waiting trap made us dress hurriedly. Stumbling about in the dark hotel room, I reached inside my travel bag for a toothbrush and jammed a finger into the corner of my razor blade, slicing a chunk of flesh clean off. Blood ran down to my elbow by the time I found something to wrap my throbbing finger. It took a while, but the bleeding finally slowed enough for a bandage, so John and I could be on our way.

As we stepped outside into the freezing cold, the wind felt like a slap in the face. It was well below zero as we jumped into the icy seats of my old Ford. But when I turned the ignition, the car wouldn't start. I cranked it again and again, but it was useless. Had to be a frozen gas line we figured, and nearby stood two lonely gas pumps. After getting a key from the hotel owner, we borrowed a half-cup and poured it down the carburetor hoping to defrost the gas line. I quickly jumped back into the driver's seat and turned the ignition key. Two whirs and a whimper was all I got. We had run down the battery while trying to start the engine. Fortunately, a passing motorist with jumper cables came to the rescue, and we were finally on our way.

As we crunched through frozen snow toward the pond, we both had very high hopes. This would be the first time in our lives that we were about to check a beaver set. Approaching, I felt my heart pounding as I took my belt ax and chopped at the fresh covering of ice. I hacked out a small opening and peered into the hole. There was no guessing, the water was as clean and clear as spring rain. The trap we had come so far and waited so long to check was empty.

But tomorrow was another day and we still had a chance for a beaver, so we made a second set by the rear of the lodge. Being slightly experienced beaver trappers now (very slightly I should say), the set went together smoother and faster than before. And as I was putting some final touches to the pole, I heard a noise: a faint crunching sound. I signaled John to listen. At first we weren't sure what to make of it, but soon realized we were listening to a beaver gnawing on its lunch inside the lodge. With high hopes for a catch, we quickly finished making our set and started back for the car.

The remainder of our afternoon was spent exploring for trapping grounds. We roamed aimlessly over countless winding back roads, but it was almost impossible to tell a frozen beaver pond from an open field with the heavy snow-cover.

As darkness approached, we found ourselves by a small pond near the road's edge. I volunteered to check it out while John stayed with the car in case another vehicle came along the narrow pass. As I walked toward the frozen pond, snowflakes the size of half-dollars began to fall lazily around me. Another squall had arrived, and soon the white flakes came in a frenzy, cutting my vision to a minimum. Squinting into the white landscape, I spotted a beaver lodge in the distance and made for it. But another trapper had already been there and completed two pole sets. This particular trapper traveled in style with a snowmobile and had a packed trail leading through a field back to the road. I followed it to my car and slid back inside with John. The two beaver sets we had would have to do. There was no time left for more.

Later that night, the roads became slippery, and by dinnertime two inches of fresh snow covered the ground with no sign of a halt. We realized this could turn into a terrific storm and hoped we wouldn't have trouble checking our traps or returning home the following day.

The next morning we were up early. I looked out the window, but it was too dark to tell the snow depth, so we hurriedly dressed and went outside. The sky was still gray but the snow had stopped. Twelve additional inches had fallen, and when the plow went through, it pushed snow over my car, burying it. I had parked against an embankment between two six-foot piles of snow, and the only way out was backwards. Making matters worse, the doors were blocked clear up to the windows and both shovels were inside. We used our feet to kick through the snow until we could open a door far enough to retrieve our shovels. After a half-hour of steady digging, we were finally on our way.

With the new snow, the roads were even narrower than before. And when our road forked left, the plow turned right. We had no choice but to dig out a parking spot for our car and walk a half mile to the pond. With the additional new powder, we had three feet of snow to dig through before finally easing the car off the road's edge.

We grabbed our packbasket and ax from the trunk and started down the snow-covered road to our pond. After pushing several hundred yards, we decided to take a shortcut across a field. Trail breaking was tough: twice we sank to our waists in drifts covering low spots, and by the time we reached the pond we were both soaked with perspiration. The shortcut hadn't been such a good idea after all.

But all our struggling was forgotten as we approached our two sets. I remembered the sound of a beaver gnawing on a branch in his lodge the day before, and I felt certain we'd have him as I chopped away at the ice above our trap. But when I peered into the water my heart fell, and I gave my brother the bad news.

We moved to our next trap, our last chance for a catch. John kneeled and broke through the frozen water surrounding it. Then he looked up. Didn't say a word. Didn't have to. I could see in his eyes that we had failed.

Later, as we bounced down the country road toward the highway and home, I began to reminisce about all the great days we'd had on our traplines in the past. And I was certain more were to come. I wondered if my twin brother felt the same way, and was about to ask, when he turned his head toward me. "I know what you're thinking, Bill," he said. "We have plenty of days on the trapline ahead and plenty more furs to stretch. After all, this was only our first time for beaver."

The author with muskrats, coon, and fox, circa 1971

In the Company of Children

I HAD JUST FINISHED loading my truck with traps when I felt a gentle tug on my coattail and turned. My six-year-old son was staring up at me. "Daddy, can I go with you?" he asked urgently.

The first day of muskrat season was at hand, and it promised to be busy. I had assured a local greenskeeper that I'd liberate his golf course from these pesky rodents, and my time was limited. Taking a child along would only slow me down, and I almost said no. But when I looked into my son's pleading eyes my heart began to melt.

"Think you can keep up?" I asked with an easy smile.

Jesse nodded in short, woodpecker strokes. "Yes, Daddy," he beamed. "I can help you carry the traps!" Then he spun around and dashed into the house. "Mommy!" he squealed. "I'm going trapping with Daddy and I need my coat!"

It was a Saturday morning, back in 1987, and as much as I enjoyed running a trapline, I had to admit that after 25 years, the excitement was beginning to wear off a bit. Oh, I still loved reading animal sign and matching wits with wild critters on their own turf. But the intense, heart-pounding thrill of discovering a muskrat, coon, or fox in one of my traps had faded considerably over the years. Little did I know that my universe was about to change.

Driving toward the golf course, sitting side by side, I could sense Jesse's mounting excitement as he stared at the countryside rushing by his window and dreamed about the adventures awaiting him on the trapline. His enthusiasm was contagious, and suddenly I couldn't wait to get started.

Pulling into the country club, I eased my truck around a maintenance building and parked behind it. It was a brilliant autumn day of rich blue skies and white puffy clouds as I grabbed my packbasket from the truck's bed and motioned Jesse to follow me. "C'mon, partner," I called. "Let's go set some traps."

My target area consisted of four half-acre ponds fed by a narrow stream that snaked through the fairways. Many beautiful plants and shrubs decorated the playing area, which at first glance seemed lush and pristine, but when we walked to the stream's edge, we found places where the bank had eroded into oblivion. "Muskrat damage!" I muttered to my son.

"Why did they do that?" he asked with a puzzled look.

"They eat the roots of grasses and other vegetation growing near the banks," I explained. "They're constantly digging for food and tunneling underground to create denning areas. Eventually, the bank starts to cave in from all their burrowing unless they're trapped out."

Jesse gazed at the stream meandering through the expansive fairway and turned to me with arched eyebrows. "Daddy," he said with a shrug of bewilderment, "I think we need a hundred traps!"

"Not quite," I chuckled. "See that grooved passage running along the bottom of the stream? That's called a run. The muskrats scour out those passages with their hind feet from repeated trips up and down the stream. We're going to place traps in the runs every so often; that way we'll catch most of the muskrats as they travel from pond to pond."

Jesse watched intently as I pulled a bodygripping trap and two wooden stakes from my packbasket and waded into the stream. After centering the trap on the bottom of the run with its spring sticking straight up, I slipped the stakes through the spring's eye in crisscross fashion, anchoring them into the streambed just outside the trap's jaws. The two stakes formed an X, with the bottom half serving as guide posts while the top half encouraged the muskrat to dive under them into the trap.

I continued setting traps in similar fashion until we reached the first pond. Here Jesse and I scouted for submerged den entrances, and when we found one I would set the trap and hand it to Jesse by the chain so he could lower it into the water to settle in front of a den. Then I'd stake it solid and we would move to the next spot.

By the time we emptied the packbasket and started back to my truck it was late afternoon, and Jesse was having difficulty keeping up. I slung the packbasket over my left shoulder and crouched down. "Tired, partner?" I asked.

Jesse squinted into the sun and nodded wearily as I cradled him under my arm and stood. He snuggled close to me. "Better?" I asked softly. Nestling his head against my shoulder, he closed his eyes and hugged my neck. By the time we reached the truck he'd fallen fast asleep.

Author with son, Jesse, on the muskrat line

The following morning we were up at dawn to check our traps. I let Jesse run ahead as we approached the first set, and he dashed to the stream's edge to peer into the crystal water. "We got one, Daddy!" he cried. His face lit up like a Christmas tree as he turned toward me. "Hurry up! It's a big one!"

Now *I* was excited too. In fact, I couldn't remember the last time I felt so wound up over trapping. I hurried to the stream, removed the muskrat from the trap, and held our prize in the air, its rich brown fur glistening in the blazing sun like a fine jewel. "He's a beauty!" I crowed. "An absolute beauty." Jesse clapped his hands and jumped up and down with glee. And I became a kid again, by golly. Just like my son. And it felt wonderful!

We continued checking traps until we finished the morning with 14 plump muskrats before heading back to the truck. When we arrived, the greenskeeper was waiting for us.

"How'd you do?" he asked in a gravely voice.

I set the packbasket down and dumped our catch at his feet. "We should have just as many again tomorrow," I said.

The greenskeeper folded his heavy arms across his chest and smiled. "Can't tell you how much I appreciate this. They've been wreaking havoc with my fairways all summer long." Then he pursed his lips and squinted hard at me. "Don't suppose you can catch coyotes too?" he said. "Got some on my farm; I need 'em trapped out."

Coyotes were extremely rare in Pennsylvania back then. I had never even seen one before, and I leaped at the opportunity. "I'll give it a try," I said. "How about we follow you over right now and set some traps?"

It was a short drive to the farm, and since my time was limited, I only set two traps. I found coyote droppings along a farm lane and made two dirt hole sets nearby, making sure prevailing winds would carry my lure toward the fields beyond.

The next morning I awoke before the alarm clock rang and peered out my bedroom window. Snow had been in the forecast and I was delighted to see two inches of fresh white powder. The storm would increase our chances of catching a coyote, and I couldn't wait to check our traps. Tiptoeing into Jesse's bedroom, I discovered he too was awake, so after a hurried breakfast we jumped in the truck and started toward the farm.

Driving along the snow-covered jeep trail toward our traps, we spotted a dead deer in the distance and circled over to investigate. Coyote tracks were everywhere, but they had eaten too much of the carcass to determine how it had been killed. "Think we caught one of them?" Jesse asked.

"Hope so," I said. "Our first set is just ahead."

We continued on, and after rounding a bend, came face to face with a huge coyote in our trap. "We got one!" I cried. Jesse gaped in owlish disbelief as the shaggy beast crouched low and leered at us with yellow, predatory eyes. At a good 40 pounds, the animal equaled him in weight.

After dispatching the coyote, I remade the set and took another one the following morning. Jesse and I caught a bunch of muskrats that day too, and we continued to trap together for many years to come.

But as my son grew into a teenager, his interest in cars and girls began to take precedence over trapping with his dad. Thankfully, my daughter took an interest in trapping at about the same time. I remember her standing in the cold garage at the tender age of nine as I stepped in with a muskrat I'd caught. "Daddy, can I pet it?" she asked with wide, eager eyes.

"Sure, honey," I said. And as I watched Sarah caress the supple fur with her little hand, I was reminded how much fun it would be to have a child with me on the trapline again. "Want to check some traps tomorrow morning?" I asked.

Sarah looked up at me and shook her head briskly. "Yes, Daddy!" she breathed.

Snow cover was deep and the wind icy cold as we pulled a dozen traps from a frozen stream the following morning. They were all empty, which made Sarah begin to wonder if I really knew anything at all about trapping.

"How many traps do you have, Daddy?" She asked, her tone indicating concern.

"Five more to go," I said with a reassuring smile. "Two muskrat sets and three for beaver." Then I knelt by her side and told her that I didn't know if we'd catch any muskrats because it was the last day of the season, and I had been trapping here for several days. She was clearly disappointed with the news, and my heart sank.

The two muskrat traps were in a small ice-covered pond, and as we approached, I instructed her to wait on the bank while I walked out to them. When I reached the traps, I could see two prime muskrats had been snagged, and though I'd caught hundreds before, I was thrilled by my discovery. After chopping through the ice, I yanked the furry carcasses from the water and held them over my head like a silly schoolboy. "Surprise!" I cried.

Sarah giggled with delight as I walked over and handed one of the muskrats to her. "Help me carry our catch, partner," I said.

By now we were both chilled to the bone, so we shuffled quickly through the snow until we reached my truck and climbed inside. I started the engine, turned the heat on full blast, and looked over at my daughter. "Cold, huh?"

Sarah clicked her feet together to knock the snow off her boots and shoved her hands into her coat. "Brrrr!" she said with a shivery smile.

I nodded in agreement. "Well, it's official," I declared. "You're a real, honest-to-goodness trapper now."

"Just like Daddy?"

"Yep! Just like Daddy. And by the time we reach the beaver pond you'll be all warmed up again. Promise."

"You too, Daddy?" Sarah asked with a level of concern uncommon for a child her age.

"Me? Oh, I'm already warm," I said. "Just by having you in the truck with me." And I watched her innocent face soften with relief as she settled back to gaze at the passing countryside.

My beaver sets consisted of three bodygripping traps placed into a run in a warm spring that refused to ice over. Although the trap jaws filled the run from side to side, all three traps had to be propped up so the upper jaws were jutting above the water line, which would encourage the beavers to duck under them. Each trap had been set in exactly the same manner, with a fresh poplar limb placed behind them as an added attractant.

As we pulled into the farm, I glanced over at Sarah. The snow from her boots now a tiny puddle below her feet. "I saw fresh tracks yesterday when I set my traps. They were from a big beaver."

"How big?"

"Almost as big as you," I said.

Sarah's eyes flashed. "As big as me!"

"Yep."

And as I eased my truck along the pond's edge, I peeked over my daughter's shoulder while she hurriedly pulled on her mittens. Floating below us were three large beavers, one in each of my traps. "C'mon, honey," I said, shutting down the engine. "Let's go see if we caught anything . . . "

Although many seasons have come and gone since those early days, I can still remember them as if they were only yesterday. They are cherished memories, etched in my soul forever. Days when the sun seemed warmer, the snow a little brighter, and the fur so much richer, simply because a child was there.

Author and daughter, Sarah, with 3 beavers

About the Author

William Wasserman served as secretary of the Pennsylvania Trappers Association in 1973 but gave up the position when he started his career with the Pennsylvania Game Commission the following year. While serving as a wildlife conservation officer, he received the Pennsylvania Trappers Association Presidential Award in 2006 in recognition of his continued dedication to the sport. He retired from the Game Commission after thirty-two years of dedicated service. Wasserman is a prolific writer who has been published in dozens of national magazines including *The Trapper and Predator Caller, Fur-Fish-Game, Pennsylvania Game News, International Game Warden, South Carolina Wildlife,* and *The Alberta Game Warden.* He has written six books about his life as a state game warden.

Made in the USA
Columbia, SC
08 December 2024

48703709R00074